© Scripture Union 2003
ISBN Single 1 84427 034 3
Pack of ten 1 84427 033 5

Contemporary English Version © American Bible Society 1991, 1992, 1995
Used by permisssion/Anglicisations © British & Foreign Bible Society 1997

Scripture Union, 207–209 Queensway, Bletchley, MK2 2EB, UK
Email: info@scriptureunion.org.uk
Website: www.scriptureunion.org.uk

Scripture Union Australia, Locked Bag 2, Central Coast Business Centre, NSW
2252
Website: www.su.org.au

Scripture Union USA, PO Box 987, Valley Forge, PA 19482
Website: www.scriptureunion.org

Title: Xpedition Force Matthew's Story EPS 2005 / 10K

Cover design by Kevin Wade
Typesetting in Germany by MAWPIX
Printed in Italy by Lego S.p.a.

Scripture Union is an international Christian charity working in more
than 130 countries in church and school situations, providing resources,
training and educational opportunities.
In the UK, Scripture Union has a network of volunteers, staff and associates,
who run holidays, church-based events, lead assemblies, take RE lessons and
facilitate school Christian groups. The Publishing division publishes a range of
fiction and Bible information books for children and young people, as well as
resources for teachers and those working in a school environment. For further
details contact www.scriptureunion.org.uk

## This is to certify that

_____

## has joined Xpedition Force at

_____

## Date _____

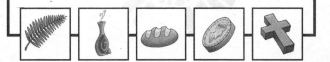

**Collect the names or doodles of the Xplorers who went with you on the Xpedition...**

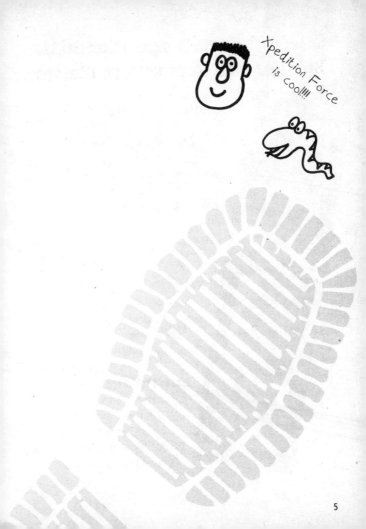

Xpedition Force is cool!!!!

# Xpedition factfile on Matthew

**Name:** Matthew, also known as Levi

**Dad's name:** Alphaeus

**Job:** Tax collector

**Home:** Galilee, North Israel

**Famous for:** Being a follower of Jesus and writing one of the four Gospels

**What others thought of him:**
Unpopular because tax collectors were known as cheats who worked for the Romans. But Jesus wanted him as a friend.

**Reason for writing:** He wanted followers of Jesus to obey God and live good lives.
He wanted people to hear about Jesus' teaching and the story of his life and death.

# Xpedition factfile on Matthew's Gospel

**Chapters:** 28

**Verses:** 1071

**Longest chapter:** 26

**Shortest chapters:** 1,3 and 28

**Number of parables/stories Jesus told:** 15

**Number of miracles Jesus did:** 19 (as well as the times when Jesus healed lots of people altogether. Jesus coming alive again was the greatest miracle of all!)

Mark, Luke and John also wrote about Jesus but in a slightly different way!

Matthew tells the good news

**CHAPTER 26**
**The plot to kill Je**
This is also told in Mark 14:1,2; Luke 22:1,2;

1 When Jesus had fir
his disciples, 2 "You
now will be Passov
Man will be hang
d to a cross

**CHAPTER 13**
**A story about a**
is also told in Mark 4:1–9; Luke 8:4-8

hat same day, Jesus le
wn out beside Lake G
wn to teach.* 2 Such l
nd him that he had
eople stood on th

**CHAPTER 9**
**esus heals a cri**
his is also told in Mark 2:1–12; Luke 5:17–2

Jesus got into a boat
he town where he li
prought to him a crip
When Jesus saw how
aid to the crippled
orry! Your sins are

**e plot to**
also told in Mark 14:1,2;

When Jesus

# Where to find
# Xpedition Force stories

# How to use
# Xpedition Force Matthew's Story

Matthew's story is also known as Matthew's Gospel. It is the first book in the New Testament part of the Bible. It's broken up into 28 chapters. The chapter number is the big black number you see on the left of a page.

Each chapter is split into sections which have been given a heading. These are then split into smaller verses. The verse numbers are the small numbers that appear in the story.

For example, you can read about Jesus riding into Jerusalem in:

# Matthew 21:1–11

Find the big number 21 (which is on page 76). The section heading is 'Jesus enters Jerusalem'.

The story begins at the beginning of the page (we think you know that the chapter begins at verse 1, so the first little number you see is 2!). The story ends at verse 11 on the next page.

## The ancestors and birth of Jesus
### The ancestors of Jesus

**1** Jesus Christ came from the family of King David and also from the family of Abraham. And this is a list of his ancestors. [2-6a]From Abraham to King David, his ancestors were:

Abraham, Isaac, Jacob, Judah and his brothers (Judah's sons were Perez and Zerah, and their mother was Tamar), Hezron;

Ram, Amminadab, Nahshon, Salmon, Boaz (his mother was Rahab), Obed (his mother was Ruth), Jesse, and King David.

[6b-11]From David to the time of the exile in Babylonia, the ancestors of Jesus were:

David, Solomon (his mother had been Uriah's wife), Rehoboam, Abijah, Asa, Jehoshaphat, Jehoram;

Uzziah, Jotham, Ahaz, Hezekiah, Manasseh, Amon, Josiah, and Jehoiachin and his brothers.

[12-16]From the exile to the birth of Jesus, his ancestors were:

Jehoiachin, Shealtiel, Zerubbabel, Abiud, Eliakim, Azor, Zadok, Achim;

Eliud, Eleazar, Matthan, Jacob, and Joseph, the husband of Mary, the mother of Jesus, who is called the Messiah.

[17]There were fourteen generations from Abraham to David. There were also fourteen from David to the exile in Babylonia and fourteen more to the birth of the Messiah.

### The birth of Jesus

[18]This is how Jesus Christ was born. A young woman named Mary was engaged to Joseph from King David's family. But

before they were married, she learnt that she was going to have a baby by God's Holy Spirit. [19]Joseph was a good man and did not want to embarrass Mary in front of everyone. So he decided to call off the wedding quietly.

[20]While Joseph was thinking about this, an angel from the Lord came to him in a dream. The angel said, "Joseph, the baby that Mary will have is from the Holy Spirit. Go ahead and marry her. [21]Then after her baby is born, name him Jesus, because he will save his people from their sins."

[22]So the Lord's promise came true, just as the prophet had said, [23]"A virgin will have a baby boy, and he will be called Immanuel, " which means "God is with us."

[24]After Joseph woke up, he and Mary were soon married, just as the Lord's angel had told him to do. [25]But they did not sleep together before her baby was born. Then Joseph named him Jesus.

### The wise men

2 When Jesus was born in the village of Bethlehem in Judea, Herod was king. During this time some wise men from the east came to Jerusalem [2]and said, "Where is the child born to be king of the Jews? We saw his star in the east and have come to worship him."

[3]When King Herod heard about this, he was worried, and so was everyone else in Jerusalem. [4]Herod brought together the chief priests and the teachers of the Law of Moses and asked them, "Where will the Messiah be born?"

[5]They told him, "He will be born in Bethlehem, just as the

prophet wrote,

> [6]"Bethlehem in the land   of Judea,
>> you are very important
>>> among the towns of Judea.
>> From your town
>>> will come a leader,
>> who will be like a shepherd
>>> for my people Israel."

[7]Herod secretly called in the wise men and asked them when they had first seen the star. [8]He told them, "Go to Bethlehem and search carefully for the child. As soon as you find him, let me know. I want to go and worship him too."

[9]The wise men listened to what the king said and then left. And the star they had seen in the east went on ahead of them until it stopped over the place where the child was. [10]They were thrilled and excited to see the star.

[11]When the men went into the house and saw the child with Mary, his mother, they knelt down and worshipped him. They took out their gifts of gold, frankincense, and myrrh and gave them to him. [12]Later they were warned in a dream not to return to Herod, and they went back home by another road.

## The escape to Egypt

[13]After the wise men had gone, an angel from the Lord appeared to Joseph in a dream and said, "Get up! Hurry and take the child and his mother to Egypt! Stay there until I tell you to return, because Herod is looking for the child and wants to kill him."

¹⁴That night, Joseph got up and took his wife and the child to Egypt, ¹⁵where they stayed until Herod died. So the Lord's promise came true, just as the prophet had said, "I called my son out of Egypt."

## The killing of the children

¹⁶When Herod found out that the wise men from the east had tricked him, he was very angry. He gave orders for his men to kill all the boys who lived in or near Bethlehem and were two years old and younger. This was based on what he had learnt from the wise men.

¹⁷So the Lord's promise came true, just as the prophet Jeremiah had said,

¹⁸"In Ramah a voice was heard
        crying and weeping loudly.
    Rachel was mourning
        for her children,
    and she refused
    to be comforted,
        because they were dead."

## The return from Egypt

¹⁹After King Herod died, an angel from the Lord appeared in a dream to Joseph while he was still in Egypt. ²⁰The angel said, "Get up and take the child and his mother back to Israel. The people who wanted to kill him are now dead."

²¹Joseph got up and left with them for Israel. ²²But when he heard that Herod's son Archelaus was now ruler of Judea, he

was afraid to go there. Then in a dream he was told to go to Galilee, [23]and they went to live there in the town of Nazareth. So the Lord's promise came true, just as the prophet had said, "He will be called a Nazarene."

### The message of John the Baptist
#### The preaching of John the Baptist

**3** Years later, John the Baptist started preaching in the desert of Judea. [2]He said, "Turn back to God! The kingdom of heaven will soon be here."

[3]John was the one the prophet Isaiah was talking about, when he said,

> "In the desert someone
>     is shouting,
> 'Get the road ready
>     for the Lord!
> Make a straight path
>     for him. "

[4]John wore clothes made of camel's hair. He had a leather strap around his waist and ate grasshoppers and wild honey.

[5]From Jerusalem and all Judea and from the River Jordan Valley crowds of people went to John. [6]They told how sorry they were for their sins, and he baptized them in the river.

[7]Many Pharisees and Sadducees also came to be baptized. But John said to them:

You snakes! Who warned you to run from the coming judgment? [8]Do something to show that you have really given up your sins. [9]And don't start telling yourselves that you belong to

Abraham's family. I tell you that God can turn these stones into children for Abraham. ¹⁰An axe is ready to cut the trees down at their roots. Any tree that doesn't produce good fruit will be chopped down and thrown into a fire.

¹¹I baptize you with water so that you will give up your sins. But someone more powerful is going to come, and I am not good enough even to carry his sandals. He will baptize you with the Holy Spirit and with fire. ¹²His threshing fork is in his hand, and he is ready to separate the wheat from the husks. He will store the wheat in a barn and burn the husks in a fire that never goes out.

## The baptism and temptation of Jesus
### The baptism of Jesus

¹³Jesus left Galilee and went to the River Jordan to be baptized by John. ¹⁴But John kept objecting and said, "I ought to be baptized by you. Why have you come to me?"

¹⁵Jesus answered, "For now this is how it should be, because we must do all that God wants us to do." Then John agreed.

¹⁶So Jesus was baptized. And as soon as he cáme out of the water, the sky opened, and he saw the Spirit of God coming down on him like a dove. ¹⁷Then a voice from heaven said, "This is my own dear Son, and I am pleased with him."

### Jesus and the devil

**4** The Holy Spirit led Jesus into the desert, so that the devil could test him. ²After Jesus had gone without eating for forty days and nights, he was very hungry. ³Then the devil came

to him and said, "If you are God's Son, tell these stones to turn
into bread."

⁴Jesus answered, "The Scriptures say:

> 'No one can live only on food.
> People need every word
>     that God has spoken. "

⁵Next, the devil took Jesus to the holy city and made him
stand on the highest part of the temple.⁶The devil said, "If you
are God's Son, jump off. The Scriptures say:

> 'God will give his angels
>     orders about you.
> They will catch you
>     in their arms,
> and you won't hurt
>     your feet on the stones. "

⁷Jesus answered, "The Scriptures also say, 'Don't try to test
the Lord your God!' "

⁸Finally, the devil took Jesus up on a very high mountain and
showed him all the kingdoms on earth and their power. ⁹The
devil said to him, "I will give all this to you, if you will bow down
and worship me."

¹⁰Jesus answered, "Go away Satan! The Scriptures say:

> 'Worship the Lord your God
>     and serve only him. "

¹¹Then the devil left Jesus, and angels came to help him.

## Jesus in Galilee
### Jesus begins his work

[12]When Jesus heard that John had been put in prison, he went to Galilee. [13]But instead of staying in Nazareth, Jesus moved to Capernaum. This town was beside Lake Galilee in the territory of Zebulun and Naphtali. [14]So God's promise came true, just as the prophet Isaiah had said,

[15]"Listen, lands of Zebulun
    and Naphtali,
lands along the road
to the sea
and east
    of the Jordan!
Listen Galilee,
    land of the Gentiles!
[16] Although your people
    live in darkness,
they will see
    a bright light.
Although they live
    in the shadow of death,
a light will shine
    on them."

[17]Then Jesus started preaching, "Turn back to God! The kingdom of heaven will soon be here."

## Jesus chooses four fishermen

[18]While Jesus was walking along the shore of Lake Galilee, he saw two brothers. One was Simon, also known as Peter, and the other was Andrew. They were fishermen, and they were casting their net into the lake. [19]Jesus said to them, "Come with me! I will teach you how to bring in people instead of fish." [20]At once the two brothers dropped their nets and went with him.

[21]Jesus walked on until he saw James and John, the sons of Zebedee. They were in a boat with their father, mending their nets. Jesus asked them to come with him too. [22]Straight away they left the boat and their father and went with Jesus.

## Jesus teaches, preaches, and heals

[23]Jesus went all over Galilee, teaching in the Jewish meeting places and preaching the good news about God's kingdom. He also healed every kind of disease and sickness. [24]News about him spread all over Syria, and people with every kind of sickness or disease were brought to him. Some of them had a lot of demons in them, others were thought to be mad, and still others could not walk. But Jesus healed them all.

[25]Large crowds followed Jesus from Galilee and the region around the ten cities known as Decapolis. They also came from Jerusalem, Judea, and from across the River Jordan.

## The sermon on the mount

**5** When Jesus saw the crowds, he went up on the side of a mountain and sat down.

**Blessings**

Jesus' disciples gathered around him, [2]and he taught them:
   [3]God blesses those people
      who depend only on him.
    They belong to the kingdom
      of heaven!
   [4]God blesses those people
    who grieve.
      They will find comfort!
   [5]God blesses those people
    who are humble.
    The earth will belong
      to them!
   [6]God blesses those people
    who want to obey him
      more than to eat or drink.
    They will be given
      what they want!
   [7]God blesses those people
    who are merciful.
    They will be treated
      with mercy!
   [8]God blesses those people
    whose hearts are pure.
      They will see him!
   [9]God blesses those people
      who make peace.

They will be called
 his children!
<sup>10</sup> God blesses those people
 who are treated badly
  for doing right.
 They belong to the kingdom
  of heaven.
<sup>11</sup>God will bless you when people insult you, ill-treat you, and tell all kinds of evil lies about you because of me. <sup>12</sup>Be happy and excited! You will have a great reward in heaven. People did these same things to the prophets who lived long ago.

## Salt and light

Jesus continued:
 <sup>13</sup>You are like salt for everyone on earth. But if salt no longer tastes like salt, how can it make food salty? All it is good for is to be thrown out and walked on.
 <sup>14</sup>You are like light for the whole world. A city built on top of a hill cannot be hidden, <sup>15</sup>and no one would light a lamp and put it under a clay pot. A lamp is placed on a lampstand, where it can give light to everyone in the house. <sup>16</sup>Make your light shine, so that others will see the good that you do and will praise your Father in heaven.

## The Law of Moses

Jesus continued:
 <sup>17</sup>Don't suppose that I came to do away with the Law and the Prophets. I did not come to do away with them, but to give them

their full meaning. [18]Heaven and earth may disappear. But I promise you that not even a full stop or comma will ever disappear from the Law. Everything written in it must happen.

[19]If you reject even the least important command in the Law and teach others to do the same, you will be the least important person in the kingdom of heaven. But if you obey and teach others its commands, you will have an important place in the kingdom. [20]You must obey God's commands better than the Pharisees and the teachers of the Law obey them. If you don't, I promise you that you will never get into the kingdom of heaven.

### Anger

Jesus continued:

[21]You know that our ancestors were told, "Do not murder" and "A murderer must be brought to trial." [22]But I promise you that if you are angry with someone, you will have to stand trial. If you call someone a fool, you will be taken to court. And if you say that someone is worthless, you will be in danger of the fires of hell.

[23]So if you are about to place your gift on the altar and remember that someone is angry with you, [24]leave your gift there in front of the altar. Make peace with that person, then come back and offer your gift to God.

[25]Before you are dragged into court, make friends with the person who has accused you of doing wrong. If you don't, you will be handed over to the judge and then to the officer who will put you in jail. [26]I promise you that you will not get out until you have paid the last penny you owe.

## Marriage

Jesus continued:

²⁷You know the commandment which says, "Be faithful in marriage." ²⁸But I tell you that if you look at another woman and want her, you are already unfaithful in your thoughts. ²⁹If your right eye causes you to sin, poke it out and throw it away. It is better to lose one part of your body, than for your whole body to end up in hell. ³⁰If your right hand causes you to sin, chop it off and throw it away! It is better to lose one part of your body, than for your whole body to be thrown into hell.

## Divorce

Jesus continued:

³¹You have been taught that a man who divorces his wife must write out divorce papers for her. ³²But I tell you not to divorce your wife unless she has committed some terrible sexual sin. If you divorce her, you will cause her to be unfaithful, just as any man who marries her is guilty of taking another man's wife.

## Promises

Jesus continued:

³³You know that our ancestors were told, "Don't use the Lord's name to make a promise unless you are going to keep it." ³⁴But I tell you not to swear by anything when you make a promise! Heaven is God's throne, so don't swear by heaven. ³⁵The earth is God's footstool, so don't swear by the earth. Jerusalem is the city of the great king, so don't swear by it.

[36]Don't swear by your own head. You cannot make one hair white or black. [37]When you make a promise, say only "Yes" or "No". Anything else comes from the devil.

## Revenge

Jesus continued:

[38]You know that you have been taught, "An eye for an eye and a tooth for a tooth." [39]But I tell you not to try to get even with a person who has done something to you. When someone slaps your right cheek, turn and let that person slap your other cheek. [40]If someone sues you for your shirt, give up your coat as well. [41]If a soldier forces you to carry his pack one kilometre, carry it two kilometres. [42]When people ask you for something, give it to them. When they want to borrow money, lend it to them.

## Love

Jesus continued:

[43]You have heard people say, "Love your neighbours and hate your enemies." [44]But I tell you to love your enemies and pray for anyone who ill-treats you. [45]Then you will be acting like your Father in heaven. He makes the sun rise on both good and bad people. And he sends rain for the ones who do right and for the ones who do wrong. [46]If you love only those people who love you, will God reward you for that? Even tax collectors love their friends. [47]If you greet only your friends, what's so great about that? Don't even unbelievers do that? [48]But you must always act like your Father in heaven.

## Giving

Jesus said:

**6** When you do good deeds, don't try to show off. If you do, you won't get a reward from your Father in heaven.

²When you give to the poor, don't blow a loud horn. That's what show-offs do in the meeting places and on the street corners, because they are always looking for praise. I can assure you that they already have their reward.

³When you give to the poor, don't let anyone know about it. ⁴Then your gift will be given in secret. Your Father knows what is done in secret, and he will reward you.

## Prayer

Jesus continued:

⁵When you pray, don't be like those show-offs who love to stand up and pray in the meeting places and on the street corners. They do this just to look good. I can assure you that they already have their reward.

⁶When you pray, go into a room alone and close the door. Pray to your Father in private. He knows what is done in private, and he will reward you.

⁷When you pray, don't talk on and on as people do who don't know God. They think God likes to hear long prayers. ⁸Don't be like them. Your Father knows what you need before you ask.

[9]You should pray like this:
>    Our Father in heaven,
>    help us to honour
>        your name.
>[10] Come and set up
>        your kingdom,
>    so that everyone on earth
>        will obey you,
>    as you are obeyed
>        in heaven.
>[11] Give us our food for today.
>[12] Forgive us for doing wrong,
>        as we forgive others.
>[13] Keep us from being tempted
>        and protect us from evil.

[14]If you forgive others for the wrongs they do to you, your Father in heaven will forgive you. [15]But if you don't forgive others, your Father will not forgive your sins.

## Worshipping God by going without eating

Jesus continued:

[16]When you go without eating, don't try to look gloomy as those show-offs do when they go without eating. I can assure you that they already have their reward. [17]Instead, comb your hair and wash your face. [18]Then others won't know that you are going without eating. But your Father sees what is done in private, and he will reward you.

## Treasures in heaven

Jesus continued:

¹⁹Don't store up treasures on earth! Moths and rust can destroy them, and thieves can break in and steal them. ²⁰Instead, store up your treasures in heaven, where moths and rust cannot destroy them, and thieves cannot break in and steal them. ²¹Your heart will always be where your treasure is.

## Light

Jesus continued:

²²Your eyes are like a window for your body. When they are good, you have all the light you need. ²³But when your eyes are bad, everything is dark. If the light inside you is dark, you are in the dark.

## Money

Jesus continued:

²⁴You cannot be the slave of two masters! You will like one more than the other or be more loyal to one than the other. You cannot serve both God and money.

## Worry

Jesus continued:

²⁵I tell you not to worry about your life. Don't worry about having something to eat, drink, or wear. Isn't life more than food or clothing? ²⁶Look at the birds in the sky! They don't plant

or harvest. They don't even store grain in barns. Yet your Father in heaven takes care of them. Aren't you worth more than birds?

27Can worry make you live longer? 28Why worry about clothes? Look how the wild flowers grow. They don't work hard to make their clothes. 29But I tell you that Solomon with all his wealth wasn't as well clothed as one of them. 30God gives such beauty to everything that grows in the fields, even though it is here today and thrown into a fire tomorrow. He will surely do even more for you! Why do you have such little faith?

31Don't worry and ask yourselves, "Will we have anything to eat? Will we have anything to drink? Will we have any clothes to wear?" 32Only people who don't know God are always worrying about such things. Your Father in heaven knows that you need all these. 33But more than anything else, put God's work first and do what he wants. Then the other things will be yours as well.

34Don't worry about tomorrow. It will take care of itself. You have enough to worry about today.

## Judging others

Jesus said:

**7** Don't condemn others, and God won't condemn you. 2God will be as hard on you as you are on others! He will treat you exactly as you treat them.

3You can see the speck in your friend's eye, but you don't notice the log in your own eye. 4How can you say, "My friend, let me take the speck out of your eye," when you don't see the log in your own eye? 5You're nothing but show-offs! First, take the log out of your own eye. Then you can see how to take the speck out of your friend's eye.

⁶Don't give to dogs what belongs to God. They will only turn and attack you. Don't throw pearls down in front of pigs. They will trample all over them.

### Ask, search, knock

Jesus continued:

⁷Ask, and you will receive. Search, and you will find. Knock, and the door will be opened for you. ⁸Everyone who asks will receive. Everyone who searches will find. And the door will be opened for everyone who knocks. ⁹Would any of you give your hungry child a stone, if the child asked for some bread? ¹⁰Would you give your child a snake if the child asked for a fish? ¹¹As bad as you are, you still know how to give good gifts to your children. But your heavenly Father is even more ready to give good things to people who ask.

¹²Treat others as you want them to treat you. This is what the Law and the Prophets are all about.

### The narrow gate

Jesus continued:

¹³Go in through the narrow gate. The gate to destruction is wide, and the road that leads there is easy to follow. A lot of people go through that gate. ¹⁴But the gate to life is very narrow. The road that leads there is so hard to follow that only a few people find it.

## A tree and its fruit

Jesus continued:

[15]Watch out for false prophets! They dress up like sheep, but inside they are wolves who have come to attack you. [16]You can tell what they are by what they do. No one picks grapes or figs from thorn bushes. [17]A good tree produces good fruit, and a bad tree produces bad fruit. [18]A good tree cannot produce bad fruit, and a bad tree cannot produce good fruit. [19]Every tree that produces bad fruit will be chopped down and burnt. [20]You can tell who the false prophets are by their deeds.

## A warning

Jesus continued:

[21]Not everyone who calls me their Lord will get into the kingdom of heaven. Only the ones who obey my Father in heaven will get in. [22]On the day of judgment many will call me their Lord. They will say, "We preached in your name, and in your name we forced out demons and performed many miracles." [23]But I will tell them, "I will have nothing to do with you! Get out of my sight, you evil people!"

## Two builders

Jesus continued:

[24]Anyone who hears and obeys these teachings of mine is like a wise person who built a house on solid rock. [25]Rain poured down, rivers flooded, and winds beat against that house. But it did not fall, because it was built on solid rock.

²⁶Anyone who hears my teachings and doesn't obey them is like a foolish person who built a house on sand. ²⁷The rain poured down, the rivers flooded, and the winds blew and beat against that house. Finally, it fell with a crash.

²⁸When Jesus finished speaking, the crowds were surprised at his teaching. ²⁹He taught them like someone with authority, and not like their teachers of the Law of Moses.

## Jesus heals a man

8 As Jesus came down the mountain, he was followed by large crowds. ²Suddenly a man with leprosy came and knelt in front of Jesus. He said, "Lord, you have the power to make me well, if only you wanted to."

³Jesus put his hand on the man and said, "I want to! Now you are well." At once the man's leprosy disappeared. ⁴Jesus told him, "Don't tell anyone about this, but go and show the priest that you are well. Then take a gift to the temple just as Moses commanded, and everyone will know that you have been healed."

## Jesus heals an army officer's servant

⁵When Jesus was going into the town of Capernaum, an army officer came up to him and said, ⁶"Lord, my servant is at home in such terrible pain that he can't even move."

⁷"I will go and heal him," Jesus replied.

⁸But the officer said, "Lord, I'm not good enough for you to come into my house. Just give the order, and my servant will get well. ⁹I have officers who give orders to me, and I have soldiers

who take orders from me. I can say to one of them, 'Go!' and he
goes. I can say to another, 'Come!' and he comes. I can say to my
servant, 'Do this!' and he will do it."

[10]When Jesus heard this, he was so surprised that he turned
and said to the crowd following him, "I tell you that in all of
Israel I've never found anyone with this much faith! [11]Many
people will come from everywhere to enjoy the feast in the
kingdom of heaven with Abraham, Isaac, and Jacob. [12]But the
ones who should have been in the kingdom will be thrown out
into the dark. They will cry and grit their teeth in pain."

[13]Then Jesus said to the officer, "You may go home now.
Your faith has made it happen."

At once his servant was healed.

### Jesus heals many people

[14]Jesus went to the home of Peter, where he found that Peter's
mother-in-law was sick in bed with fever. [15]He took her by the
hand, and the fever left her. Then she got up and served Jesus a
meal.

[16]That evening many people with demons in them were
brought to Jesus. And with only a word he forced out the evil
spirits and healed everyone who was sick.

[17] So God's promise came true, just as the prophet Isaiah had
said,

"He healed our diseases
and made us well."

## Some who wanted to go with Jesus

¹⁸When Jesus saw the crowd, he went across Lake Galilee. ¹⁹A teacher of the Law of Moses came up to him and said, "Teacher, I'll go anywhere with you!"

²⁰Jesus replied, "Foxes have dens, and birds have nests. But the Son of Man doesn't have a place to call his own."

²¹Another disciple said to Jesus, "Lord, let me wait till I bury my father."

²²Jesus answered, "Come with me, and let the dead bury their dead."

## A storm

²³After Jesus left in a boat with his disciples, ²⁴a terrible storm suddenly struck the lake, and waves started splashing into their boat.

Jesus was sound asleep, ²⁵so the disciples went over to him and woke him up. They said, "Lord, save us! We're going to drown!"

²⁶But Jesus replied, "Why are you so afraid? You don't have much faith." Then he got up and ordered the wind and the waves to calm down. And everything was calm.

²⁷The men in the boat were amazed and said, "Who is this? Even the wind and the waves obey him."

## Two men with demons in them

²⁸After Jesus had crossed the lake, he came to shore near the town of Gadara and started down the road. Two men with

demons in them came to him from the tombs. They were so fierce that no one could travel that way. $^{29}$Suddenly they shouted, "Jesus, Son of God, what do you want with us? Have you come to punish us before our time?"

$^{30}$Not far from there a large herd of pigs was feeding. $^{31}$So the demons begged Jesus, "If you force us out, please send us into those pigs!" $^{32}$Jesus told them to go, and they went out of the men and into the pigs. All at once the pigs rushed down the steep bank into the lake and drowned.

$^{33}$The people taking care of the pigs ran to the town and told everything, especially what had happened to the two men. $^{34}$Everyone in town came out to meet Jesus. When they saw him, they begged him to leave their part of the country.

## Jesus heals a crippled man

**9** Jesus got into a boat and crossed back over to the town where he lived. $^{2}$Some people soon brought to him a crippled man lying on a mat. When Jesus saw how much faith they had, he said to the crippled man, "My friend, don't worry! Your sins are forgiven."

$^{3}$Some teachers of the Law of Moses said to themselves, "Jesus must think he is God!"

$^{4}$But Jesus knew what was in their minds, and he said, "Why are you thinking such evil things? $^{5}$Is it easier for me to tell this crippled man that his sins are forgiven or to tell him to get up and walk? $^{6}$But I will show you that the Son of Man has the right to forgive sins here on earth." So Jesus said to the man, "Get up! Pick up your mat and go on home." $^{7}$The man got up and went home. [8]When the crowds saw this, they were afraid and praised God for giving such authority to people.

## Jesus chooses Matthew

[9]As Jesus was leaving, he saw a tax collector named Matthew sitting at the place for paying taxes. Jesus said to him, "Come with me." Matthew got up and went with him.

[10]Later, Jesus and his disciples were having dinner at Matthew's house. Many tax collectors and other sinners were also there. [11]Some Pharisees asked Jesus' disciples, "Why does your teacher eat with tax collectors and other sinners?"

[12]Jesus heard them and answered, "Healthy people don't need a doctor, but sick people do. [13]Go and learn what the Scriptures mean when they say, 'Instead of offering sacrifices to me, I want you to be merciful to others.' I didn't come to invite good people to be my followers. I came to invite sinners."

## People ask about going without eating

[14]One day some followers of John the Baptist came and asked Jesus, "Why do we and the Pharisees often go without eating, while your disciples never do?"

[15]Jesus answered:

The friends of a bridegroom don't go without eating while he is still with them. But the time will come when he will be taken from them. Then they will go without eating.

[16]No one uses a new piece of cloth to patch old clothes. The patch would shrink and tear a bigger hole.

¹⁷No one pours new wine into old wineskins. The wine would swell and burst the old skins. Then the wine would be lost, and the skins would be ruined. New wine must be put into new wineskins. Both the skins and the wine will then be safe.

## A dying girl and a sick woman

¹⁸While Jesus was still speaking, an official came and knelt in front of him. The man said, "My daughter has just died! Please come and place your hand on her. Then she will live again."

¹⁹Jesus and his disciples got up and went with the man.

²⁰A woman who had been bleeding for twelve years came up behind Jesus and barely touched his clothes. ²¹She had said to herself, "If I can just touch his clothes, I will get well."

²²Jesus turned. He saw the woman and said, "Don't worry! You are now well because of your faith." At that moment she was healed.

²³When Jesus went into the home of the official and saw the musicians and the crowd of mourners, ²⁴he said, "Get out of here! The little girl isn't dead. She is just asleep." Everyone started laughing at Jesus. ²⁵But after the crowd had been sent out of the house, Jesus went to the girl's bedside. He took her by the hand and helped her up.

²⁶News about this spread all over that part of the country.

## Jesus heals two blind men

²⁷As Jesus was walking along, two blind men began following him and shouting, "Son of David, have pity on us!"

²⁸After Jesus had gone indoors, the two blind men came up to him. He asked them, "Do you believe I can make you well?"

"Yes, Lord," they answered.

²⁹Jesus touched their eyes and said, "Because of your faith, you will be healed." ³⁰They were able to see, and Jesus strictly warned them not to tell anyone about him. ³¹But they left and talked about him to everyone in that part of the country.

## Jesus heals a man who could not talk

³²As Jesus and his disciples were on their way, some people brought to him a man who could not talk because a demon was in him. ³³After Jesus had forced the demon out, the man started talking. The crowds were so amazed that they began saying, "Nothing like this has ever happened in Israel!"

³⁴But the Pharisees said, "The leader of the demons gives him the power to force out demons."

## Jesus has pity on people

³⁵Jesus went to every town and village. He taught in their meeting places and preached the good news about God's kingdom. Jesus also healed every kind of disease and sickness. ³⁶When he saw the crowds, he felt sorry for them. They were confused and helpless, like sheep without a shepherd. ³⁷He said to his disciples, "A large crop is in the fields, but there are only a few workers. ³⁸Ask the Lord in charge of the harvest to send out workers to bring it in."

### Jesus chooses his twelve apostles

**10** Jesus called together his twelve disciples. He gave them the power to force out evil spirits and to heal every kind of disease and sickness. ²The first of the twelve apostles was Simon, better known as Peter. His brother Andrew was an apostle, and so were James and John, the two sons of Zebedee. ³Philip, Bartholomew, Thomas, Matthew the tax collector, James the son of Alphaeus, and Thaddaeus were also apostles. ⁴The others were Simon, known as the Eager One, and Judas Iscariot, who later betrayed Jesus.

### Instructions for the twelve apostles

⁵Jesus sent out the twelve apostles with these instructions:

Stay away from the Gentiles and don't go to any Samaritan town. ⁶Go only to the people of Israel, because they are like a flock of lost sheep. ⁷As you go, announce that the kingdom of heaven will soon be here. ⁸Heal the sick, raise the dead to life, heal people who have leprosy, and force out demons. You received without paying, now give without being paid. ⁹Don't take along any gold, silver, or copper coins. ¹⁰And don't carry a travelling bag or an extra shirt or sandals or a walking stick.

Workers deserve their food. ¹¹So when you go to a town or a village, find someone worthy enough to have you as their guest and stay with them until you leave. ¹²When you go to a home, give it your blessing of peace. ¹³If the home is deserving, let your blessing remain with them. But if the home isn't deserving, take back your blessing of peace. ¹⁴If someone won't welcome you or listen to your message, leave their home or town. And shake the dust from your feet at them. ¹⁵I promise you that the day of judgment will be easier for the towns of Sodom and Gomorrah than for that town.

## Warning about trouble

Jesus continued:

¹⁶I am sending you like lambs into a pack of wolves. So be as wise as snakes and as innocent as doves. ¹⁷Watch out for people who will take you to court and have you beaten in their meeting places. ¹⁸Because of me, you will be dragged before rulers and kings to tell them and the Gentiles about your faith. ¹⁹But when someone arrests you, don't worry about what you will say or how you will say it. At that time you will be given the words to say. ²⁰But you will not really be the one speaking. The Spirit from your Father will tell you what to say.

²¹Brothers and sisters will betray one another and have each other put to death. Parents will betray their own children, and children will turn against their parents and have them killed. ²²Everyone will hate you because of me. But if you remain faithful until the end, you will be saved. ²³When people ill-treat you in one town, hurry to another one. I promise you that before you have gone to all the towns of Israel, the Son of Man will come.

²⁴Disciples are not better than their teacher, and slaves are not better than their master. ²⁵It is enough for disciples to be like their teacher and for slaves to be like their master. If people call

the head of the family Satan, what will they say about the rest of the family?

## The one to fear

Jesus continued:

²⁶Don't be afraid of anyone! Everything that is hidden will be found out, and every secret will be known. ²⁷Whatever I say to you in the dark, you must tell in the light. And you must announce from the housetops whatever I have whispered to you. ²⁸Don't be afraid of people. They can kill you, but they cannot harm your soul. Instead, you should fear God who can destroy both your body and your soul in hell. ²⁹Aren't two sparrows sold for only a penny? But your Father knows when any one of them falls to the ground. ³⁰Even the hairs on your head are counted. ³¹So don't be afraid! You are worth much more than many sparrows.

## Telling others about Christ

Jesus continued:

³²If you tell others that you belong to me, I will tell my Father in heaven that you are my followers. ³³But if you reject me, I will tell my Father in heaven that you don't belong to me.

## Not peace, but trouble

Jesus continued:

³⁴Don't think that I came to bring peace to the earth! I came to bring trouble, not peace. ³⁵I came to turn sons against their fathers, daughters against their mothers, and daughters-in-law

against their mothers-in-law. ³⁶Your worst enemies will be in your own family.

³⁷If you love your father or mother or even your sons and daughters more than me, you are not fit to be my disciples. ³⁸And unless you are willing to take up your cross and come with me, you are not fit to be my disciples. ³⁹If you try to save your life, you will lose it. But if you give it up for me, you will find it.

## Rewards

Jesus continued:

⁴⁰Anyone who welcomes you welcomes me. And anyone who welcomes me also welcomes the one who sent me. ⁴¹Anyone who welcomes a prophet, just because that person is a prophet, will be given the same reward as a prophet. Anyone who welcomes a good person, just because that person is good, will be given the same reward as a good person. ⁴²And anyone who gives one of my most humble followers a cup of cool water, just because that person is my follower, will be rewarded.

## John the Baptist

**11** After Jesus had finished instructing his twelve disciples, he left and began teaching and preaching in the towns.

²John was in prison when he heard what Christ was doing. So John sent some of his followers ³to ask Jesus, "Are you the one we should be looking for? Or must we wait for someone else?"

⁴Jesus answered, "Go and tell John what you have heard and seen. ⁵The blind are now able to see, and the lame can walk.

People with leprosy are being healed, and the deaf can hear. The dead are raised to life, and the poor are hearing the good news. ⁶God will bless everyone who doesn't reject me because of what I do."

⁷As John's followers were going away, Jesus spoke to the crowds about John:

What sort of person did you go out into the desert to see? Was he like tall grass blown about by the wind? ⁸What kind of man did you go out to see? Was he someone dressed in fine clothes? People who dress like that live in the king's palace. ⁹What did you really go out to see? Was he a prophet? He certainly was. I tell you that he was more than a prophet. ¹⁰In the Scriptures God says about him, "I am sending my messenger ahead of you to get things ready for you." ¹¹I tell you that no one ever born on this earth is greater than John the Baptist. But whoever is least in the kingdom of heaven is greater than John.

¹²From the time of John the Baptist until now, violent people have been trying to take over the kingdom of heaven by force. ¹³All the Books of the Prophets and the Law of Moses told what was going to happen up to the time of John. ¹⁴And if you believe them, John is Elijah, the prophet you are waiting for. ¹⁵If you have ears, pay attention!

¹⁶You people are like children sitting in the market and shouting to each other,

¹⁷ "We played the flute,
     but you would not dance!
We sang a funeral song,
     but you would not mourn!"

¹⁸John the Baptist did not go around eating and drinking, and you said, "That man has a demon in him!" ¹⁹But the Son of Man goes around eating and drinking, and you say, "That man eats and drinks too much! He is even a friend of tax collectors and sinners." Yet Wisdom is shown to be right by what it does.

## The unbelieving towns

²⁰In the towns where Jesus had performed most of his miracles, the people refused to turn to God. So Jesus was upset with them and said:

²¹You people of Chorazin are in for trouble! You people of Bethsaida are in for trouble too! If the miracles that took place in your towns had happened in Tyre and Sidon, the people there would have turned to God long ago. They would have dressed in sackcloth and put ashes on their heads. ²²I tell you that on the day of judgment the people of Tyre and Sidon will get off easier than you will.

²³People of Capernaum, do you think you will be honoured in heaven? You will go down to hell! If the miracles that took place in your town had happened in Sodom, that town would still be standing. ²⁴So I tell you that on the day of judgment the people of Sodom will get off easier than you.

## Come to me and rest

²⁵At that moment Jesus said:

My Father, Lord of heaven and earth, I am grateful that you hid all this from wise and educated people and showed it to ordinary people. ²⁶Yes, Father, that is what pleased you.

²⁷My Father has given me everything, and he is the only one who knows the Son. The only one who truly knows the Father is the Son. But the Son wants to tell others about the Father, so that they can know him too.

²⁸If you are tired from carrying heavy burdens, come to me and I will give you rest. ²⁹Take the yoke I give you. Put it on your shoulders and learn from me. I am gentle and humble, and you will find rest. ³⁰This yoke is easy to bear, and this burden is light.

## A question about the Sabbath

**12** One Sabbath, Jesus and his disciples were walking through some wheat fields. His disciples were hungry and began picking and eating grains of wheat. ²Some Pharisees noticed this and said to Jesus, "Why are your disciples picking grain on the Sabbath? They are not supposed to do that!"

³Jesus answered:

You must have read what David did when he and his followers were hungry. ⁴He went into the house of God, and then they ate the sacred loaves of bread that only priests are supposed to eat. ⁵Haven't you read in the Law of Moses that the priests are allowed to work in the temple on the Sabbath? But no one says that they are guilty of breaking the law of the Sabbath. ⁶I tell you that there is something here greater than the temple. ⁷Don't you know what the Scriptures mean when they say, "Instead of offering sacrifices to me, I want you to be merciful to others"? If you knew what this means, you would not condemn these innocent disciples of mine. ⁸So the Son of Man is Lord over the Sabbath.

## A man with a crippled hand

⁹Jesus left and went into one of the Jewish meeting places, ¹⁰where there was a man whose hand was crippled. Some Pharisees wanted to accuse Jesus of doing something wrong, and they asked him, "Is it right to heal someone on the Sabbath?"

¹¹Jesus answered, "If you had a sheep that fell into a ditch on the Sabbath, wouldn't you lift it out? ¹²People are worth much more than sheep, and so it is right to do good on the Sabbath." ¹³Then Jesus told the man, "Hold out your hand." The man did, and it became as healthy as the other one.

¹⁴The Pharisees left and started making plans to kill Jesus.

## God's chosen servant

¹⁵When Jesus found out what was happening, he left there and large crowds followed him. He healed all their sick, ¹⁶but warned them not to tell anyone about him. ¹⁷So God's promise came true, just as Isaiah the prophet had said,

¹⁸ "Here is my chosen servant!
   I love him,
      and he pleases me.
   I will give him my Spirit,
   and he will bring justice
      to the nations.
¹⁹ He won't shout or yell
      or call out in the streets.

[20] He won't break off a bent reed
       or put out a dying flame,
     but he will make sure  that justice is done.
[21] All nations will place
       their hope in him."

## Jesus and the ruler of the demons

[22]Some people brought to Jesus a man who was blind and could not talk because he had a demon in him. Jesus healed the man, and then he was able to talk and see. [23]The crowds were so amazed that they asked, "Could Jesus be the Son of David?"

[24]When the Pharisees heard this, they said, "He forces out demons by the power of Beelzebul, the ruler of the demons!"

[25]Jesus knew what they were thinking, and he said to them:

Any kingdom where people fight each other will end up ruined. And a town or family that fights will soon destroy itself. [26]So if Satan fights against himself, how can his kingdom last? [27]If I use the power of Beelzebul to force out demons, whose power do your own followers use to force them out? Your followers are the ones who will judge you. [28]But when I force out demons by the power of God's Spirit, it proves that God's kingdom has already come to you. [29]How can anyone break into a strong man's house and steal his things, unless he first ties up the strong man? Then he can take everything.

[30]If you are not on my side, you are against me. If you don't gather in the harvest with me, you scatter it. [31-32]I tell you that any sinful thing you do or say can be forgiven. Even if you speak against the Son of Man, you can be forgiven. But if you speak

against the Holy Spirit, you can never be forgiven, either in this life or in the life to come.

## A tree and its fruit

Jesus continued:

<sup>33</sup>A good tree produces only good fruit, and a bad tree produces bad fruit. You can tell what a tree is like by the fruit it produces. <sup>34</sup>You are evil snakes, so how can you say anything good? Your words show what is in your hearts. <sup>35</sup>Good people bring good things out of their hearts, but evil people bring evil things out of their hearts. <sup>36</sup>I promise you that on the day of judgment, everyone will have to account for every careless word they have spoken. <sup>37</sup>On that day they will be told that they are either innocent or guilty because of the things they have said.

## A sign from heaven

<sup>38</sup>Some Pharisees and teachers of the Law of Moses said, "Teacher, we want you to show us a sign from heaven."

<sup>39</sup>But Jesus replied:

You want a sign because you are evil and won't believe! But the only sign you will get is the sign of the prophet Jonah. <sup>40</sup>He was in the stomach of a big fish for three days and nights, just as the Son of Man will be deep in the earth for three days and nights. <sup>41</sup>On the day of judgment the people of Nineveh will stand there with you and condemn you. They turned to God when Jonah preached, and yet here is something far greater than Jonah. <sup>42</sup>The Queen of the South will also stand there with you and condemn you. She travelled a long way to hear Solomon's wisdom, and yet here is something much greater than Solomon.

## Return of an evil spirit

Jesus continued:

⁴³When an evil spirit leaves a person, it travels through the desert, looking for a place to rest. But when the demon doesn't find a place, ⁴⁴it says, "I will go back to the home I left." When it gets there and finds the place empty, clean, and tidy, ⁴⁵it goes off and finds seven other evil spirits even worse than itself. They all come and make their home there, and the person ends up in a worse state than before. That's how it will be with you evil people of today.

## Jesus' mother and brothers

⁴⁶While Jesus was still speaking to the crowds, his mother and brothers came and stood outside because they wanted to talk with him. ⁴⁷Someone told Jesus, "Your mother and brothers are standing outside and want to talk with you."

⁴⁸Jesus answered, "Who is my mother and who are my brothers?" ⁴⁹Then he pointed to his disciples and said, "These are my mother and my brothers! ⁵⁰Anyone who obeys my Father in heaven is my brother or sister or mother."

## A story about a farmer

**13** That same day Jesus left the house and went out beside Lake Galilee, where he sat down to teach. ²Such large crowds gathered around him that he had to sit in a boat, while the people stood on the shore. [3]Then he taught them many things by using stories. He said:

A farmer went out to scatter seed in a field. [4]While the farmer was scattering the seed, some of it fell along the road and was eaten by birds. [5]Other seeds fell on thin, rocky ground and quickly started growing because the soil wasn't very deep. [6]But when the sun came up, the plants were scorched and dried up, because they did not have enough roots. [7]Some other seeds fell where thorn bushes grew up and choked the plants. [8]But a few seeds did fall on good ground where the plants produced a hundred or sixty or thirty times as much as was scattered. [9]If you have ears, pay attention!

## Why Jesus used stories

[10]Jesus' disciples came to him and asked, "Why do you use nothing but stories when you speak to the people?"

[11]Jesus answered:

I have explained the secrets about the kingdom of heaven to you, but not to others. [12]Everyone who has something will be given more. But people who don't have anything will lose even what little they have. [13]I use stories when I speak to them because when they look, they cannot see, and when they listen, they cannot hear or understand. [14]So God's promise came true, just as the prophet Isaiah had said,

"These people will listen
and listen,
but never understand.
They will look and look,

but never see.
<sup>15</sup> All of them have
stubborn minds!
Their ears are stopped up,
and their eyes are covered.
They cannot see or hear
or understand.
If they could,
they would turn to me,
and I would heal them."

<sup>16</sup>But God has blessed you, because your eyes can see and your ears can hear! <sup>17</sup>Many prophets and good people were eager to see what you see and to hear what you hear. But I tell you that they did not see or hear.

## Jesus explains the story about the farmer

<sup>18</sup>Now listen to the meaning of the story about the farmer:

<sup>19</sup>The seeds that fell along the road are the people who hear the message about the kingdom, but don't understand it. Then the evil one comes and snatches the message from their hearts. <sup>20</sup>The seeds that fell on rocky ground are the people who gladly hear the message and accept it straight away. <sup>21</sup>But they don't have deep roots, and they don't last very long. As soon as life gets hard or the message gets them in trouble, they give up.

<sup>22</sup>The seeds that fell among the thorn bushes are also people who hear the message. But they start worrying about the needs of this life and are fooled by the desire to get rich. So the message gets choked out, and they never produce

anything. [23]The seeds that fell on good ground are the people who hear and understand the message. They produce as much as a hundred or sixty or thirty times what was planted.

## Weeds among the wheat

[24]Jesus then told them this story:

The kingdom of heaven is like what happened when a farmer scattered good seed in a field. [25]But while everyone was sleeping, an enemy came and scattered weeds in the field and then left.

[26]When the plants came up and began to ripen, the farmer's servants could see the weeds. [27]The servants came and asked, "Sir, didn't you scatter good seed in your field? Where did these weeds come from?"

[28]"An enemy did this, " he replied.

His servants then asked, "Do you want us to go out and pull up the weeds?"

[29]"No!" he answered. "You might also pull up the wheat. [30]Leave the weeds alone until harvest time. Then I'll tell my workers to gather the weeds and tie them up and burn them. But I'll order them to store the wheat in my barn."

## Stories about a mustard seed and yeast

[31]Jesus told them another story:

The kingdom of heaven is like what happens when a farmer plants a mustard seed in a field. [32]Although it is the smallest of all seeds, it grows larger than any garden plant and becomes a tree. Birds even come and nest on its branches.

[33]Jesus also said:

The kingdom of heaven is like what happens when a woman mixes a little yeast into three big batches of flour. Finally, all the dough rises.

## The reason for teaching with stories

[34]Jesus used stories when he spoke to the people. In fact, he did not tell them anything without using stories.
[35] So God's promise came true, just as the prophet had said,
   "I will use stories
       to speak my message
   and to explain things
       that have been hidden
   since the creation
       of the world."

## Jesus explains the story about the weeds

[36]After Jesus left the crowd and went inside, his disciples came to him and said, "Explain to us the story about the weeds in the wheat field."
[37]Jesus answered:

The one who scattered the good seed is the Son of Man. [38]The field is the world, and the good seeds are the people who belong to the kingdom. The weeds are those who belong to the evil one, [39]and the one who scattered them is the devil. The harvest is the end of time, and angels are the ones who bring in the harvest.

[40]Weeds are gathered and burnt. That's how it will be at the end of time. [41]The Son of Man will send out his angels, and they will gather from his kingdom everyone who does wrong or causes others to sin. [42]Then he will throw them into a flaming furnace, where people will cry and grit their teeth in pain. [43]But everyone who has done right will shine like the sun in their Father's kingdom. If you have ears, pay attention!

**A hidden treasure**

Jesus continued:

[44]The kingdom of heaven is like what happens when someone finds treasure hidden in a field and buries it again. A person like that is happy and goes and sells everything in order to buy that field.

**A valuable pearl**

Jesus continued:

[45]The kingdom of heaven is like what happens when a shop owner is looking for fine pearls. [46]After finding a very valuable one, the owner goes and sells everything in order to buy that pearl.

**A fish net**

Jesus continued:

[47]The kingdom of heaven is like what happens when a net is thrown into a lake and catches all kinds of fish. [48]When the net is full, it is dragged to the shore, and the fishermen sit down to separate the fish. They keep the good ones, but throw the bad

ones away. [49]That's how it will be at the end of time. Angels will come and separate the evil people from the ones who have done right. [50]Then those evil people will be thrown into a flaming furnace, where they will cry and grit their teeth in pain.

## New and old treasures

[51]Jesus asked his disciples if they understood all these things. They said, "Yes, we do."

[52]So he told them, "Every student of the Scriptures who becomes a disciple in the kingdom of heaven is like someone who brings out new and old treasures from the storeroom."

## The people of Nazareth turn against Jesus

[53]When Jesus had finished telling these stories, he left [54]and went to his home town. He taught in their meeting place, and the people were so amazed that they asked, "Where does he get all this wisdom and the power to perform these miracles? [55]Isn't he the son of the carpenter? Isn't Mary his mother, and aren't James, Joseph, Simon, and Judas his brothers? [56]Don't his sisters still live here in our town? How can he do all this?" [57]So the people were very unhappy because of what he was doing.

But Jesus said, "Prophets are honoured by everyone, except the people of their home town and their own family." [58]And because the people did not have any faith, Jesus did not perform many miracles there.

## The death of John the Baptist

**14** About this time Herod the ruler heard the news about Jesus ²and told his officials, "This is John the Baptist! He has come back from death, and that's why he has the power to perform these miracles."

³⁻⁴Herod had earlier arrested John and had him chained and put in prison. He did this because John had told him, "It isn't right for you to take Herodias, the wife of your brother Philip." ⁵Herod wanted to kill John. But the people thought John was a prophet, and Herod was afraid of what they might do.

⁶When Herod's birthday came, the daughter of Herodias danced for the guests. She pleased Herod ⁷so much that he swore to give her whatever she wanted. ⁸But the girl's mother told her to say, "Here on a dish I want the head of John the Baptist!"

⁹The king was sorry for what he had said. But he did not want to break the promise he had made in front of his guests. So he ordered a guard ¹⁰to go to the prison and cut off John's head. ¹¹It was taken on a dish to the girl, and she gave it to her mother. ¹²John's followers took his body and buried it. Then they told Jesus what had happened.

## Jesus feeds five thousand

¹³After Jesus heard about John, he crossed Lake Galilee to go to some place where he could be alone. But the crowds found out and followed him on foot from the towns. ¹⁴When Jesus got

out of the boat, he saw the large crowd. He felt sorry for them and healed everyone who was sick.

[15]That evening the disciples came to Jesus and said, "This place is like a desert, and it is already late. Let the crowds leave, so they can go to the villages and buy some food."

[16]Jesus replied, "They don't have to leave. Why don't you give them something to eat?"

[17]But they said, "We have only five small loaves of bread and two fish." [18]Jesus asked his disciples to bring the food to him, [19]and he told the crowd to sit down on the grass. Jesus took the five loaves and the two fish. He looked up towards heaven and blessed the food. Then he broke the bread and handed it to his disciples, and they gave it to the people.

[20]After everyone had eaten all they wanted, Jesus' disciples picked up twelve large baskets of leftovers.

[21]There were about five thousand men who ate, not counting the women and children.

### Jesus walks on the water

[22]Straight away, Jesus made his disciples get into a boat and start back across the lake. But he stayed until he had sent the crowds away. [23]Then he went up on a mountain where he could be alone and pray. Later that evening, he was still there.

[24]By this time the boat was a long way from the shore. It was going against the wind and was being tossed around by the waves. [25]A little while before morning, Jesus came walking on the water towards his disciples. [26]When they saw him, they

thought he was a ghost. They were terrified and started screaming.

²⁷At once, Jesus said to them, "Don't worry! I am Jesus. Don't be afraid."

²⁸Peter replied, "Lord, if it is really you, tell me to come to you on the water."

²⁹"Come on!" Jesus said. Peter then got out of the boat and started walking on the water towards him.

³⁰But when Peter saw how strong the wind was, he was afraid and started sinking. "Save me, Lord!" he shouted.

³¹Straight away, Jesus reached out his hand. He helped Peter up and said, "You don't have much faith. Why do you doubt?"

³²When Jesus and Peter got into the boat, the wind died down. ³³The men in the boat worshipped Jesus and said, "You really are the Son of God!"

## Jesus heals sick people in Gennesaret

³⁴Jesus and his disciples crossed the lake and came to shore near the town of Gennesaret. ³⁵The people found out that he was there, and they sent word to everyone who lived in that part of the country. So they brought all the sick people to Jesus. ³⁶They begged him just to let them touch his clothes, and everyone who did was healed.

## The teaching of the ancestors

**15** About this time some Pharisees and teachers of the Law of Moses came from Jerusalem. They asked Jesus,

²"Why don't your disciples obey what our ancestors taught us to do? They don't even wash their hands before they eat."

³Jesus answered:

Why do you disobey God and follow your own teaching? ⁴Didn't God command you to respect your father and mother? Didn't he tell you to put to death all who curse their parents? ⁵But you let people get by without helping their parents when they should. You let them say that what they have has been offered to God. ⁶Is this any way to show respect to your parents? You ignore God's commands in order to follow your own teaching. ⁷And you are nothing but show-offs! Isaiah the prophet was right when he wrote that God had said,

⁸ "All of you praise me
　　with your words,
　but you never really
　　think about me.
⁹ It is useless for you
　　to worship me,
　when you teach rules
　　made up by humans."

## What really makes people unclean

¹⁰Jesus called the crowd together and said, "Pay attention and try to understand what I mean. ¹¹The food that you put into your mouth doesn't make you unclean and unfit to worship God. The bad words that come out of your mouth are what make you unclean."

¹²Then his disciples came over to him and asked, "Do you know that you insulted the Pharisees by what you said?"

¹³Jesus answered, "Every plant that my Father in heaven did not plant will be pulled up by the roots. ¹⁴Stay away from those Pharisees! They are like blind people leading other blind people, and all of them will fall into a ditch."

¹⁵Peter replied, "What did you mean when you talked about the things that make people unclean?"

¹⁶Jesus then said:

Don't any of you know what I am talking about by now? ¹⁷Don't you know that the food you put into your mouth goes into your stomach and then out of your body? ¹⁸But the words that come out of your mouth come from your heart. And they are what make you unfit to worship God. ¹⁹Out of your heart come evil thoughts, murder, unfaithfulness in marriage, vulgar deeds, stealing, telling lies, and insulting others. ²⁰These are what make you unclean. Eating without washing your hands will not make you unfit to worship God.

## A woman's faith

²¹Jesus left and went to the territory near the cities of Tyre and Sidon. ²²Suddenly a Canaanite woman from there came out shouting, "Lord and Son of David, have pity on me! My daughter is full of demons." ²³Jesus did not say a word. But the woman kept following along and shouting, so his disciples came up and asked him to send her away.

²⁴Jesus said, "I was sent only to the people of Israel! They are like a flock of lost sheep."

[25]The woman came closer. Then she knelt down and begged, "Please help me, Lord!"

[26]Jesus replied, "It isn't right to take food away from children and feed it to dogs."

[27]"Lord, that's true," the woman said, "but even dogs get the crumbs that fall from their owner's table."

[28]Jesus answered, "Dear woman, you really do have a lot of faith, and you will be given what you want." At that moment her daughter was healed.

## Jesus heals many people

[29]From there, Jesus went along Lake Galilee. Then he climbed a hill and sat down. [30]Large crowds came and brought many people who were crippled or blind or lame or unable to talk. They placed them, and many others, in front of Jesus, and he healed them all. [31]Everyone was amazed at what they saw and heard. People who had never spoken could now speak. The lame were healed, the crippled could walk, and the blind were able to see. Everyone was praising the God of Israel.

## Jesus feeds four thousand

[32]Jesus called his disciples together and told them, "I feel sorry for these people. They have been with me for three days, and they don't have anything to eat. I don't want to send them away hungry. They might faint on their way home."

[33]His disciples said, "This place is like a desert. Where can we find enough food to feed such a crowd?"

[34]Jesus asked them how much food they had. They replied, "Seven small loaves of bread and a few little fish."

[35]After Jesus had told the people to sit down, [36]he took the seven loaves of bread and the fish and gave thanks. He then broke them and handed them to his disciples, who passed them around to the crowds.

[37]Everyone ate all they wanted, and the leftovers filled seven large baskets.

[38]There were four thousand men who ate, not counting the women and children.

[39]After Jesus had sent the crowds away, he got into a boat and sailed across the lake. He came to shore near the town of Magadan.

## A demand for a sign from heaven

**16** The Pharisees and Sadducees came to Jesus and tried to test him by asking for a sign from heaven. [2]He told them:

If the sky is red in the evening, you say the weather will be good. [3]But if the sky is red and gloomy in the morning, you say it is going to rain. You can tell what the weather will be like by looking at the sky. But you don't understand what is happening now. [4]You want a sign because you are evil and won't believe! But the only sign you will be given is what happened to Jonah.

Then Jesus left.

## The yeast of the Pharisees and Sadducees

[5]The disciples had forgotten to bring any bread when they crossed the lake. [6]Jesus then warned them, "Watch out! Guard against the yeast of the Pharisees and Sadducees."

[7]The disciples talked this over and said to each other, "He must be saying this because we didn't bring along any bread."

[8]Jesus knew what they were thinking and said:

You don't have much faith! Why are you talking about not having any bread? [9]Don't you understand? Have you forgotten about the five thousand people and all those baskets of leftovers from just five loaves of bread? [10]And what about the four thousand people and all those baskets of leftovers from only seven loaves of bread? [11]Don't you know by now that I am not talking to you about bread? Watch out for the yeast of the Pharisees and Sadducees!

[12]Finally, the disciples understood that Jesus wasn't talking about the yeast used to make bread, but about the teaching of the Pharisees and Sadducees.

## Who is Jesus?

[13]When Jesus and his disciples were near the town of Caesarea Philippi, he asked them, "What do people say about the Son of Man?"

[14]The disciples answered, "Some people say you are John the Baptist or perhaps Elijah or Jeremiah or some other prophet."

[15]Then Jesus asked them, "But who do you say I am?"

[16]Simon Peter spoke up, "You are the Messiah, the Son of the living God."

[17]Jesus told him:

Simon, son of Jonah, you are blessed! You didn't discover this on your own. It was shown to you by my Father in heaven. [18]So I will call you Peter, which means "a rock". On this rock I will build my church, and death itself will not have any power over it. [19]I will give you the keys to the kingdom of heaven, and God in heaven will allow whatever you allow on earth. But he will not allow anything that you don't allow.

[20]Jesus told his disciples not to tell anyone that he was the Messiah.

## Jesus speaks about his suffering and death

[21]From then on, Jesus began telling his disciples what would happen to him. He said, "I must go to Jerusalem. There the nation's leaders, the chief priests, and the teachers of the Law of Moses will make me suffer terribly. I will be killed, but three days later I will rise to life."

[22]Peter took Jesus aside and told him to stop talking like that. He said, "God would never let this happen to you, Lord!"

[23]Jesus turned to Peter and said, "Satan, get away from me! You're in my way because you think like everyone else and not like God."

[24]Then Jesus said to his disciples:

If any of you want to be my followers, you must forget about yourself. You must take up your cross and follow me. [25]If you want to save your life, you will destroy it. But if you give up your life for me, you will find it. ²⁶What will you gain, if you own the whole world but destroy yourself? What would you give to get back your soul?

²⁷The Son of Man will soon come in the glory of his Father and with his angels to reward all people for what they have done. ²⁸I promise you that some of those standing here will not die before they see the Son of Man coming with his kingdom.

## The true glory of Jesus

**17** Six days later Jesus took Peter and the brothers James and John with him. They went up on a very high mountain where they could be alone. ²There in front of the disciples, Jesus was completely changed. His face was shining like the sun, and his clothes became white as light.

³All at once Moses and Elijah were there talking with Jesus. ⁴So Peter said to him, "Lord, it is good for us to be here! Let us make three shelters, one for you, one for Moses, and one for Elijah."

⁵While Peter was still speaking, the shadow of a bright cloud passed over them. From the cloud a voice said, "This is my own dear Son, and I am pleased with him. Listen to what he says!" ⁶When the disciples heard the voice, they were so afraid that they fell flat on the ground. ⁷But Jesus came over and touched them. He said, "Get up and don't be afraid!" ⁸When they opened their eyes, they saw only Jesus.

⁹On their way down from the mountain, Jesus warned his disciples not to tell anyone what they had seen until after the Son of Man had been raised from death.

¹⁰The disciples asked Jesus, "Don't the teachers of the Law of Moses say that Elijah must come before the Messiah does?"

¹¹Jesus told them, "Elijah certainly will come and get everything ready. ¹²In fact, he has already come. But the people did not recognize him and treated him just as they wanted to. They will soon make the Son of Man suffer in the same way." ¹³Then the disciples understood that Jesus was talking to them about John the Baptist.

## Jesus heals a boy

¹⁴Jesus and his disciples returned to the crowd. A man knelt in front of him ¹⁵and said, "Lord, have pity on my son! He has a bad case of epilepsy and often falls into a fire or into water. ¹⁶I brought him to your disciples, but none of them could heal him."

¹⁷Jesus said, "You people are too stubborn to have any faith! How much longer must I be with you? Why do I have to put up with you? Bring the boy here." ¹⁸Then Jesus spoke sternly to the demon. It went out of the boy, and at once he was healed.

¹⁹Later the disciples went to Jesus in private and asked him, "Why couldn't we force out the demon?"

²⁰⁻²¹Jesus replied:

It is because you don't have enough faith! But I can promise you this. If you had faith no larger than a mustard seed, you could tell this mountain to move from here to there. And it would. Everything would be possible for you.

### Jesus again speaks about his death

²²While Jesus and his disciples were going from place to place in Galilee, he told them, "The Son of Man will be handed over to people ²³who will kill him. But three days later he will rise to life." All this made the disciples very sad.

### Paying the temple tax

²⁴When Jesus and the others arrived in Capernaum, the collectors for the temple tax came to Peter and asked, "Does your teacher pay the temple tax?"

²⁵"Yes, he does," Peter answered.

After they had returned home, Jesus went up to Peter and asked him, "Simon, what do you think? Do the kings of this earth collect taxes and fees from their own people or from foreigners?"

²⁶Peter answered, "From foreigners."

Jesus replied, "Then their own people don't have to pay. ²⁷But we don't want to cause trouble. So go and cast a line into the lake and pull out the first fish you hook. Open its mouth, and you will find a coin. Use it to pay your taxes and mine."

### Who is the greatest?

**18** About this time the disciples came to Jesus and asked him who would be the greatest in the kingdom of heaven. ²Jesus called a child over and made the child stand near him. ³Then he said:

I promise you this. If you don't change and become like a child, you will never get into the kingdom of heaven. ⁴But if you are as humble as this child, you are the greatest in the kingdom of heaven. ⁵And when you welcome one of these children because of me, you welcome me.

## Temptations to sin

Jesus continued:
⁶It will be terrible for people who cause even one of my little followers to sin. Those people would be better off thrown into the deepest part of the sea with a heavy stone tied around their necks! ⁷The world is in for trouble because of the way it causes people to sin. There will always be something to cause people to sin, but anyone who does this will be in for trouble.

⁸If your hand or foot causes you to sin, chop it off and throw it away! You would be better off to go into life crippled or lame than to have two hands or two feet and be thrown into the fire that never goes out. ⁹If your eye causes you to sin, poke it out and get rid of it. You would be better off to go into life with only one eye than to have two eyes and be thrown into the fires of hell.

## The lost sheep

Jesus continued:
¹⁰⁻¹¹Don't be cruel to any of these little ones! I promise you that their angels are always with my Father in heaven. ¹²Let me ask you this. What would you do if you had a hundred sheep and one of them wandered off? Wouldn't you leave the ninety-nine

on the hillside and go and look for the one that had wandered away? $^{13}$I am sure that finding it would make you happier than having the ninety-nine that never wandered off. $^{14}$That's how it is with your Father in heaven. He doesn't want any of these little ones to be lost.

## When someone sins

Jesus continued:

$^{15}$If one of my followers sins against you, go and point out what was wrong. But do it in private, just between the two of you. If that person listens, you have won back a follower. $^{16}$But if that one refuses to listen, take along one or two others. The Scriptures teach that every complaint must be proved true by two or more witnesses. $^{17}$If the follower refuses to listen to them, report the matter to the church. Anyone who refuses to listen to the church must be treated like an unbeliever or a tax collector.

## Allowing and not allowing

Jesus continued:

$^{18}$I promise you that God in heaven will allow whatever you allow on earth, but he will not allow anything you don't allow. $^{19}$I promise that when any two of you on earth agree about something you are praying for, my Father in heaven will do it for you. $^{20}$Whenever two or three of you come together in my name, I am there with you.

## An official who refused to forgive

²¹Peter came up to the Lord and asked, "How many times should I forgive someone who does something wrong to me? Is seven times enough?"

²²Jesus answered:

Not just seven times, but seventy-seven times! ²³This story will show you what the kingdom of heaven is like:

One day a king decided to call in his officials and ask them to give an account of what they owed him. ²⁴As he was doing this, one official was brought in who owed him fifty million silver coins. ²⁵But he didn't have any money to pay what he owed. The king ordered him to be sold, along with his wife and children and all he owned, in order to pay the debt.

²⁶The official got down on his knees and began begging, "Have pity on me, and I will pay you every penny I owe!" ²⁷The king felt sorry for him and let him go free. He even told the official that he did not have to pay back the money.

²⁸As the official was leaving, he happened to meet another official, who owed him a hundred silver coins. So he grabbed the man by the throat. He started choking him and said, "Pay me what you owe!"

²⁹The man got down on his knees and began begging, "Have pity on me, and I will pay you back." ³⁰But the first official refused to have pity. Instead, he went and had the other official put in jail until he could pay what he owed.

³¹When some other officials found out what had happened, they felt sorry for the man who had been put in jail. Then they

told the king what had happened. <sup>32</sup>The king called the first
official back in and said, "You're an evil man! When you begged
for mercy, I said you did not have to pay back a penny. <sup>33</sup>Don't
you think you should show pity to someone else, as I did to
you?" <sup>34</sup>The king was so angry that he ordered the official to be
tortured until he could pay back everything he owed. <sup>35</sup>That is
how my Father in heaven will treat you, if you don't forgive each
of my followers with all your heart.

## Jesus goes from Galilee to Jerusalem
### Teaching about divorce

**19** When Jesus finished teaching, he left Galilee and went to
the part of Judea that is east of the River Jordan. <sup>2</sup>Large
crowds followed him, and he healed their sick people.

<sup>3</sup>Some Pharisees wanted to test Jesus. They came up to him
and asked, "Is it right for a man to divorce his wife for just any
reason?"

<sup>4</sup>Jesus answered, "Don't you know that in the beginning the
Creator made a man and a woman? <sup>5</sup>That's why a man leaves
his father and mother and gets married. He becomes like one
person with his wife. <sup>6</sup>Then they are no longer two people, but
one. And no one should separate a couple that God has joined
together."

<sup>7</sup>The Pharisees asked Jesus, "Why did Moses say that a man
could write out divorce papers and send his wife away?"

<sup>8</sup>Jesus replied, "You are so heartless! That's why Moses
allowed you to divorce your wife. But from the beginning God
did not intend it to be that way. <sup>9</sup>I say that if your wife has not

committed some terrible sexual sin, you must not divorce her to marry someone else. If you do, you are unfaithful."

[10]The disciples said, "If that's how it is between a man and a woman, it's better not to get married."

[11]Jesus told them, "Only those people who have been given the gift of staying single can accept this teaching. [12]Some people are unable to marry because of birth defects or because of what someone has done to their bodies. Others stay single for the sake of the kingdom of heaven. Anyone who can accept this teaching should do so."

## Jesus blesses little children

[13]Some people brought their children to Jesus, so that he could place his hands on them and pray for them. His disciples told the people to stop bothering him. [14]But Jesus said, "Let the children come to me, and don't try to stop them! People who are like these children belong to God's kingdom." [15]After Jesus had placed his hands on the children, he left.

## A rich young man

[16]A man came to Jesus and asked, "Teacher, what good thing must I do to have eternal life?"

[17]Jesus said to him, "Why do you ask me about what is good? Only God is good. If you want to have eternal life, you must obey his commandments."

[18]"Which ones?" the man asked.

Jesus answered, "Do not murder. Be faithful in marriage. Do not steal. Do not tell lies about others. [19]Respect your father and mother. And love others as much as you love yourself." [20]The young man said, "I have obeyed all these. What else must I do?"

[21]Jesus replied, "If you want to be perfect, go and sell everything you own! Give the money to the poor, and you will have riches in heaven. Then come and be my follower." [22]When the young man heard this, he was sad, because he was very rich.

[23]Jesus said to his disciples, "It's terribly hard for rich people to get into the kingdom of heaven! [24]In fact, it's easier for a camel to go through the eye of a needle than for a rich person to get into God's kingdom."

[25]When the disciples heard this, they were greatly surprised and asked, "How can anyone ever be saved?"

[26]Jesus looked straight at them and said, "There are some things that people cannot do, but God can do anything."

[27]Peter replied, "Remember, we have left everything to be your followers! What will we get?"

[28]Jesus answered:

Yes, all of you have become my followers. And so in the future world, when the Son of Man sits on his glorious throne, I promise that you will sit on twelve thrones to judge the twelve tribes of Israel. [29]All who have given up home or brothers and sisters or father and mother or children or land for me will be given a hundred times as much. They will also have eternal life. [30]But many who are now first will be last, and many who are last will be first.

## Workers in a vineyard

**20** As Jesus was telling what the kingdom of heaven would be like, he said:

Early one morning a man went out to hire some workers for his vineyard. ²After he had agreed to pay them the usual amount for a day's work, he sent them off to his vineyard.

³About nine that morning, the man saw some other people standing in the market with nothing to do. ⁴He said he would pay them what was fair, if they would work in his vineyard. ⁵So they went.

At midday and again about three in the afternoon he returned to the market. And each time he made the same agreement with others who were lazing around with nothing to do.

⁶Finally, about five in the afternoon the man went back and found some others standing there. He asked them, "Why have you been standing here all day long doing nothing?"

⁷"Because no one has hired us," they answered. Then he told them to go and work in his vineyard.

⁸That evening the owner of the vineyard told the man in charge of the workers to call them in and give them their money. He also told the man to begin with the ones who were hired last. ⁹When the workers arrived, the ones who had been hired at five in the afternoon were given a full day's pay.

¹⁰The workers who had been hired first thought they would be given more than the others. But when they were given the same, ¹¹they began complaining to the owner of the vineyard. ¹²They said, "The ones who were hired last worked for

only one hour. But you paid them the same that you did us. And we worked in the hot sun all day long!"

[13]The owner answered one of them, "Friend, I didn't cheat you. I paid you exactly what we agreed on. [14]Take your money now and go! What business is it of yours if I want to pay them the same that I paid you? [15]Don't I have the right to do what I want with my own money? Why should you be jealous, if I want to be generous?"

[16]Jesus then said, "So it is. Everyone who is now first will be last, and everyone who is last will be first."

## Jesus again tells about his death

[17]As Jesus was on his way to Jerusalem, he took his twelve disciples aside and told them in private:

[18]We are now on our way to Jerusalem, where the Son of Man will be handed over to the chief priests and the teachers of the Law of Moses. They will sentence him to death, [19]and then they will hand him over to foreigners who will make fun of him. They will beat him and nail him to a cross. But on the third day he will rise from death.

## A mother's request

[20]The mother of James and John came to Jesus with her two sons. She knelt down and started begging him to do something for her. [21]Jesus asked her what she wanted, and she said, "When you come into your kingdom, please let one of my sons sit at your right side and the other at your left."

²²Jesus answered, "Not one of you knows what you are asking. Are you able to drink from the cup that I must soon drink from?"

James and John said, "Yes, we are!"

²³Jesus replied, "You certainly will drink from my cup! But it isn't for me to say who will sit at my right side and at my left. That is for my Father to say."

²⁴When the ten other disciples heard this, they were angry with the two brothers. ²⁵But Jesus called the disciples together and said:

You know that foreign rulers like to order their people around. And their great leaders have full power over everyone they rule. ²⁶But don't act like them. If you want to be great, you must be the servant of all the others. ²⁷And if you want to be first, you must be the slave of the rest. ²⁸The Son of Man did not come to be a slave master, but a slave who will give his life to rescue many people.

## Jesus heals two blind men

²⁹Jesus was followed by a large crowd as he and his disciples were leaving Jericho. ³⁰Two blind men were sitting beside the road. And when they heard that Jesus was coming their way, they shouted, "Lord and Son of David, have pity on us!"

³¹The crowd told them to be quiet, but they shouted even louder, "Lord and Son of David, have pity on us!"

³²When Jesus heard them, he stopped and asked, "What do you want me to do for you?"

³³They answered, "Lord, we want to see!"

34Jesus felt sorry for them and touched their eyes. Straight away they could see, and they became his followers.

## Jesus' last week: his trial and death
### Jesus enters Jerusalem

**21** When Jesus and his disciples came near Jerusalem, he went to Bethphage on the Mount of Olives and sent two of them on ahead. 2He told them, "Go into the next village, where you will at once find a donkey and her colt. Untie the two donkeys and bring them to me. 3If anyone asks why you are doing that, just say, 'The Lord needs them.'" Straight away he will let you have the donkeys."

4So God's promise came true, just as the prophet had said,

5 "Announce to the people
    of Jerusalem:
'Your king is coming to you!
He is humble
    and rides on a donkey.
He comes on the colt
    of a donkey.'"

6The disciples left and did what Jesus had told them to do. 7They brought the donkey and its colt and laid some clothes on their backs. Then Jesus got on.

8Many people spread clothes in the road, while others put down branches which they had cut from trees. 9Some people walked ahead of Jesus and others followed behind. They were all shouting,

"Hooray for the Son of David!

God bless the one who comes
   in the name of the Lord.
   Hooray for God
      in heaven above!"

[10]When Jesus came to Jerusalem, everyone in the city was excited and asked, "Who can this be?"

[11]The crowd answered, "This is Jesus, the prophet from Nazareth in Galilee."

## Jesus in the temple

[12]Jesus went into the temple and chased out everyone who was selling or buying. He turned over the tables of the moneychangers and the benches of the ones who were selling doves. [13]He told them, "The Scriptures say, 'My house should be called a place of worship. ' But you have turned it into a place where robbers hide."

[14]Blind and lame people came to Jesus in the temple, and he healed them. [15]But the chief priests and the teachers of the Law of Moses were angry when they saw his miracles and heard the children shouting praises to the Son of David. [16]The men said to Jesus, "Don't you hear what those children are saying?"

"Yes, I do!" Jesus answered. "Don't you know that the Scriptures say, 'Children and infants will sing praises?'" [17]Then Jesus left the city and went out to the village of Bethany, where he spent the night.

## Jesus puts a curse on a fig tree

[18]When Jesus got up the next morning, he was hungry. He started out for the city, [19]and along the way he saw a fig tree. But when he came to it, he found only leaves and no figs. So he told the tree, "You will never again grow any fruit!" At once the fig tree dried up.

[20]The disciples were shocked when they saw how quickly the tree had dried up. [21]But Jesus said to them, "If you have faith and don't doubt, I promise that you can do what I did to this tree. And you will be able to do even more. You can tell this mountain to get up and jump into the sea, and it will. [22]If you have faith when you pray, you will be given whatever you ask for."

## A question about Jesus' authority

[23]Jesus had gone into the temple and was teaching when the chief priests and the leaders of the people came up to him. They asked, "What right do you have to do these things? Who gave you this authority?"

[24]Jesus answered, "I have just one question to ask you. If you answer it, I will tell you where I got the right to do these things. [25]Who gave John the right to baptize? Was it God in heaven or merely some human being?"

They thought it over and said to each other, "We can't say that God gave John this right. Jesus will ask us why we didn't believe John. [26]On the other hand, these people think that John was a prophet, and we are afraid of what they might do to us. That's why we can't say that it was merely some human who gave John the right to baptize." ²⁷So they told Jesus, "We don't know."

Jesus said, "Then I won't tell you who gave me the right to do what I do."

## A story about two sons

²⁸Jesus said:

I will tell you a story about a man who had two sons. Then you can tell me what you think. The father went to the elder son and said, "Go and work in the vineyard today!" ²⁹His son told him that he would not do it, but later he changed his mind and went. ³⁰The man then told his younger son to go and work in the vineyard. The boy said he would, but he didn't go. ³¹Which one of the sons obeyed his father?

"The elder one, " the chief priests and leaders answered.

Then Jesus told them:

You can be sure that tax collectors and prostitutes will get into the kingdom of God before you ever will! ³²When John the Baptist showed you how to do right, you would not believe him. But these evil people did believe. And even when you saw what they did, you still would not change your minds and believe.

## Tenants of a vineyard

³³Jesus told the chief priests and leaders to listen to this story:

A land owner once planted a vineyard. He built a wall around it and dug a pit to crush the grapes in. He also built a lookout tower. Then he let his vineyard and left the country.

³⁴When it was harvest time, the owner sent some servants to get his share of the grapes. ³⁵But the tenants grabbed those servants. They beat up one, killed one, and stoned one of them to death. ³⁶He then sent more servants than he did the first time. But the tenants treated them in the same way.

³⁷Finally, the owner sent his own son to the tenants, because he thought they would respect him. ³⁸But when they saw the man's son, they said, "Some day he will own the vineyard. Let's kill him! Then we can have it all for ourselves." ³⁹So they grabbed him, threw him out of the vineyard, and killed him.

⁴⁰Jesus asked, "When the owner of that vineyard comes, what do you suppose he will do to those tenants?"

⁴¹The chief priests and leaders answered, "He will kill them in some horrible way. Then he will let his vineyard to people who will give him his share of grapes at harvest time."

⁴²Jesus replied, "Surely you know that the Scriptures say,

'The stone that the builders
        tossed aside
    is now the most important
        stone of all.
    This is something
    the Lord has done,
        and it is amazing to us. '

⁴³I tell you that God's kingdom will be taken from you and given to people who will do what he demands. ⁴⁴Anyone who stumbles over this stone will be crushed, and anyone it falls on will be smashed to pieces."

[45]When the chief priests and the Pharisees heard these stories, they knew that Jesus was talking about them. [46]So they looked for a way to arrest Jesus. But they were afraid to, because the people thought he was a prophet.

## The great banquet

**22** Once again Jesus used stories to teach the people: [2]The kingdom of heaven is like what happened when a king gave a wedding banquet for his son. [3]The king sent some servants to tell the invited guests to come to the banquet, but the guests refused. [4]He sent other servants to say to the guests, "The banquet is ready! My cattle and prize calves have all been prepared. Everything is ready. Come to the banquet!"

[5]But the guests did not pay any attention. Some of them left for their farms, and some went to their places of business. [6]Others grabbed the servants, then beat them up and killed them.

[7]This made the king so furious that he sent an army to kill those murderers and burn down their city. [8]Then he said to the servants, "It is time for the wedding banquet, and the invited guests don't deserve to come. [9]Go out to the street corners and tell everyone you meet to come to the banquet."

[10]They went out into the streets and brought in everyone they could find, good and bad alike. And the banquet room was filled with guests.

[11]When the king went in to meet the guests, he found that one of them wasn't wearing the right kind of clothes for the

wedding. [12]The king asked, "Friend, why didn't you wear proper clothes for the wedding?" But the guest had no excuse. [13]So the king gave orders for that person to be tied hand and foot and to be thrown outside into the dark. That's where people will cry and grit their teeth in pain. [14]Many are invited, but only a few are chosen.

## Paying taxes

[15]The Pharisees got together and planned how they could trick Jesus into saying something wrong. [16]They sent some of their followers and some of Herod's followers to say to him, "Teacher, we know that you are honest. You teach the truth about what God wants people to do. And you treat everyone with the same respect, no matter who they are. [17]Tell us what you think! Should we pay taxes to the Emperor or not?"

[18]Jesus knew their evil thoughts and said, "Why are you trying to test me? You show-offs! [19]Let me see one of the coins used for paying taxes." They brought him a silver coin, [20]and he asked, "Whose picture and name are on it?"

[21]"The Emperor's, " they answered.

Then Jesus told them, "Give the Emperor what belongs to him and give God what belongs to God." [22]His answer surprised them so much that they walked away.

## Life in the future world

[23]The Sadducees did not believe that people would rise to life after death. So that same day some of the Sadducees came to Jesus and said:

<sup>24</sup>Teacher, Moses wrote that if a married man dies and has no children, his brother should marry the widow. Their first son would then be thought of as the son of the dead brother.

<sup>25</sup>Once there were seven brothers who lived here. The first one married, but died without having any children. So his wife was left to his brother. <sup>26</sup>The same thing happened to the second and third brothers and finally to all seven of them. <sup>27</sup>At last the woman died. <sup>28</sup>When God raises people from death, whose wife will this woman be? She had been married to all seven brothers.

<sup>29</sup>Jesus answered:

You are completely wrong! You don't know what the Scriptures teach. And you don't know anything about the power of God. <sup>30</sup>When God raises people to life, they won't marry. They will be like the angels in heaven. <sup>31</sup>And as for people being raised to life, God was speaking to you when he said, <sup>32</sup>"I am the God worshipped by Abraham, Isaac, and Jacob." He isn't the God of the dead, but of the living.

<sup>33</sup>The crowds were surprised to hear what Jesus was teaching.

## The most important commandment

<sup>34</sup>After Jesus had made the Sadducees look foolish, the Pharisees heard about it and got together. <sup>35</sup>One of them was an expert in the Jewish Law. So he tried to test Jesus by asking, <sup>36</sup>"Teacher, what is the most important commandment in the Law?"

<sup>37</sup>Jesus answered:

Love the Lord your God with all your heart, soul, and mind.
[38]This is the first and most important commandment. [39]The
second most important commandment is like this one. And it is,
"Love others as much as you love yourself." [40]All the Law of
Moses and the Books of the Prophets are based on these two
commandments.

## About David's son

[41]While the Pharisees were still there, Jesus asked them,
[42]"What do you think about the Messiah? Whose family will he
come from?"

They answered, "He will be a son of King David."

[43]Jesus replied, "How then could the Spirit lead David to call
the Messiah his Lord? David said,

[44] 'The Lord said to my Lord:
    Sit at my right side
  until I make your enemies
    into a footstool for you. '

[45]If David called the Messiah his Lord, how can the Messiah
be a son of King David?" [46]No one was able to give Jesus an
answer, and from that day on, no one dared ask him any more
questions.

## Jesus condemns the Pharisees and the teachers of the Law of Moses

**23** Jesus said to the crowds and to his disciples:
[2]The Pharisees and the teachers of the Law are experts in
the Law of Moses. [3]So obey everything they teach you, but don't

do as they do. After all, they say one thing and do something else.

⁴They pile heavy burdens on people's shoulders and won't lift a finger to help. ⁵Everything they do is just to show off in front of others. They even make a big show of wearing Scripture verses on their foreheads and arms, and they wear big tassels for everyone to see. ⁶They love the best seats at banquets and the front seats in the meeting places. ⁷And when they are in the market, they like to have people greet them as their teachers.

⁸But none of you should be called a teacher. You have only one teacher, and all of you are like brothers and sisters. ⁹Don't call anyone on earth your father. All of you have the same Father in heaven. ¹⁰None of you should be called the leader. The Messiah is your only leader. ¹¹Whoever is the greatest should be the servant of the others. ¹²If you put yourself above others, you will be put down. But if you humble yourself, you will be honoured.

¹³⁻¹⁴You Pharisees and teachers of the Law of Moses are in for trouble! You're nothing but show-offs. You lock people out of the kingdom of heaven. You won't go in yourselves, and you keep others from going in.

¹⁵You Pharisees and teachers of the Law of Moses are in for trouble! You're nothing but show-offs. You travel over land and sea to win one follower. And when you have done so, you make that person twice as fit for hell as you are.

¹⁶You are in for trouble! You are supposed to lead others, but you are blind. You teach that it doesn't matter if a person swears by the temple. But you say that it does matter if someone swears

by the gold in the temple. [17]You blind fools! Which is greater, the gold or the temple that makes the gold sacred?

[18]You also teach that it doesn't matter if a person swears by the altar. But you say that it does matter if someone swears by the gift on the altar. [19]Are you blind? Which is more important, the gift or the altar that makes the gift sacred? [20]Anyone who swears by the altar also swears by everything on it. [21]And anyone who swears by the temple also swears by God, who lives there. [22]To swear by heaven is the same as swearing by God's throne and by the one who sits on that throne. Jesus continued:

[23]You Pharisees and teachers are show-offs, and you're in for trouble! You give God a tenth of the spices from your garden, such as mint, dill, and cumin. Yet you neglect the more important matters of the Law, such as justice, mercy, and faithfulness. These are the important things you should have done, though you should not have left the others undone either. [24]You blind leaders! You strain out a small fly but swallow a camel.

[25]You Pharisees and teachers are show-offs, and you're in for trouble! You wash the outside of your cups and dishes, while inside there is nothing but greed and selfishness. [26]You blind Pharisee! First clean the inside of a cup, and then the outside will also be clean.

[27]You Pharisees and teachers are in for trouble! You're nothing but show-offs. You're like tombs that have been whitewashed. On the outside they are beautiful, but inside they are full of bones and filth. [28]That's what you are like. Outside you look good, but inside you are evil and only pretend to be good.

<sup>29</sup>You Pharisees and teachers are nothing but show-offs, and you're in for trouble! You build monuments for the prophets and decorate the tombs of good people. <sup>30</sup>And you claim that you would not have taken part with your ancestors in killing the prophets. <sup>31</sup>But you prove that you really are the relatives of the ones who killed the prophets. <sup>32</sup>So keep on doing everything they did. <sup>33</sup>You are nothing but snakes and the children of snakes! How can you escape going to hell?

<sup>34</sup>I will send prophets and wise people and experts in the Law of Moses to you. But you will kill them or nail them to a cross or beat them in your meeting places or chase them from town to town. <sup>35</sup>That's why you will be held guilty for the murder of every good person, beginning with the good man Abel. This also includes Barachiah's son Zechariah, the man you murdered between the temple and the altar. <sup>36</sup>I can promise that you people living today will be punished for all these things!

## Jesus loves Jerusalem

Jesus continued:

<sup>37</sup>Jerusalem, Jerusalem! Your people have killed the prophets and have stoned the messengers who were sent to you. I have often wanted to gather your people, as a hen gathers her chicks under her wings. But you wouldn't let me. <sup>38</sup>And now your temple will be deserted.

<sup>39</sup> You won't see me again until you say,
   "Blessed is the one who comes
   in the name of the Lord."

## The temple will be destroyed

**24** After Jesus left the temple, his disciples came over and said, "Look at all these buildings!"

²Jesus replied, "Do you see these buildings? They will certainly be torn down! Not one stone will be left in place."

## Warning about trouble

³Later, as Jesus was sitting on the Mount of Olives, his disciples came to him in private and asked, "When will this happen? What will be the sign of your coming and of the end of the world?"

⁴Jesus answered:

Don't let anyone fool you. ⁵Many will come and claim to be me. They will say that they are the Messiah, and they will fool many people.

⁶You will soon hear about wars and threats of wars, but don't be afraid. These things will have to happen first, but that isn't the end. ⁷Nations and kingdoms will go to war against each other. People will starve to death, and in some places there will be earthquakes. ⁸But this is just the beginning of troubles.

⁹You will be arrested, punished, and even killed. Because of me, you will be hated by people of all nations. ¹⁰Many will give up and will betray and hate each other. ¹¹Many false prophets will come and fool a lot of people. ¹²Evil will spread and cause many people to stop loving others. ¹³But if you keep on being faithful right to the end, you will be saved. ¹⁴When the good

news about the kingdom has been preached all over the world
and told to all nations, the end will come.

## The Horrible Thing

Jesus continued:

15Some day you will see that "Horrible Thing" in the holy
place, just as the prophet Daniel said. Everyone who reads this
must try to understand! 16If you are living in Judea at that time,
run to the mountains. 17If you are on the roof of your house,
don't go inside to get anything. 18If you are out in the field, don't
go back for your coat. 19It will be a terrible time for women who
are expecting babies or nursing young children. 20And pray that
you won't have to escape in winter or on a Sabbath. 21This will be
the worst time of suffering since the beginning of the world, and
nothing this terrible will ever happen again. 22If God doesn't
make the time shorter, no one will be left alive. But because of
God's chosen ones, he will make the time shorter.

23Someone may say, "Here is the Messiah!" or "There he is!"
But don't believe it. 24False messiahs and false prophets will
come and perform great miracles and signs. They will even try
to fool God's chosen ones. 25But I have warned you
beforehand. 26If you are told that the Messiah is out in the desert,
don't go there! And if you are told that he is in some secret place,
don't believe it! 27The coming of the Son of Man will be like
lightning that can be seen from east to west. 28Where there is a
corpse, there will always be vultures.

## When the Son of Man appears

Jesus continued:

<sup>29</sup>Straight after those days of suffering,

"The sun will become dark,
and the moon
will no longer shine.
The stars will fall,
and the powers in the sky
will be shaken."

<sup>30</sup>Then a sign will appear in the sky. And there will be the Son of Man. All nations on earth will weep when they see the Son of Man coming on the clouds of heaven with power and great glory. <sup>31</sup>At the sound of a loud trumpet, he will send his angels to bring his chosen ones together from all over the earth.

## A lesson from a fig tree

Jesus continued:

<sup>32</sup>Learn a lesson from a fig tree. When its branches sprout and start putting out leaves, you know that summer is near. <sup>33</sup>So when you see all these things happening, you will know that the time has almost come. <sup>34</sup>I can promise you that some of the people of this generation will still be alive when all this happens. <sup>35</sup>The sky and the earth won't last for ever, but my words will.

## No one knows the day or time

Jesus continued:

[36]No one knows the day or hour. The angels in heaven don't know, and the Son himself doesn't know. Only the Father knows. [37]When the Son of Man appears, things will be just as they were when Noah lived. [38]People were eating, drinking, and getting married right up to the day that the flood came and Noah went into the big boat. [39]They didn't know anything was happening until the flood came and swept them all away. That is how it will be when the Son of Man appears.

[40]Two men will be in the same field, but only one will be taken. The other will be left. [41]Two women will be together grinding grain, but only one will be taken. The other will be left. [42]So be on your guard! You don't know when your Lord will come. [43]Homeowners never know when a thief is coming, and they are always on guard to keep one from breaking in. [44]Always be ready! You don't know when the Son of Man will come.

## Faithful and unfaithful servants

Jesus continued:

[45]Who are faithful and wise servants? Who are the ones the master will put in charge of giving the other servants their food supplies at the proper time? [46]Servants are fortunate if their master comes and finds them doing their job. [47]You may be sure that a servant who is always faithful will be put in charge of everything the master owns. [48]But suppose one of the servants thinks that the master won't return until late. [49]Suppose that evil

servant starts beating the other servants and eats and drinks with people who are drunk. ⁵⁰If that happens, the master will come on a day and at a time when the servant least expects him. ⁵¹That servant will then be punished and thrown out with the ones who only pretended to serve their master. There they will cry and grit their teeth in pain.

### A story about ten girls

Jesus said:

**25** The kingdom of heaven is like what happened one night when ten girls took their oil lamps and went to a wedding to meet the groom. ²Five of the girls were foolish and five were wise. ³The foolish ones took their lamps, but no extra oil. ⁴The ones who were wise took along extra oil for their lamps.

⁵The groom was late arriving, and the girls became drowsy and fell asleep. ⁶Then in the middle of the night someone shouted, "Here's the groom! Come to meet him!"

⁷When the girls got up and started getting their lamps ready, ⁸the foolish ones said to the others, "Let us have some of your oil! Our lamps are going out."

⁹The girls who were wise answered, "There's not enough oil for all of us! Go and buy some for yourselves."

¹⁰While the foolish girls were on their way to get some oil, the groom arrived. The girls who were ready went into the wedding, and the doors were closed. ¹¹Later the other girls returned and shouted, "Sir, sir! Open the door for us!"

¹²But the groom replied, "I don't even know you!"

¹³So, my disciples, always be ready! You don't know the day or the time when all this will happen.

## A story about three servants

Jesus continued:

¹⁴The kingdom is also like what happened when a man went away and put his three servants in charge of all he owned. ¹⁵The man knew what each servant could do. So he handed five thousand coins to the first servant, two thousand to the second, and one thousand to the third. Then he left the country.

¹⁶As soon as the man had gone, the servant with the five thousand coins used them to earn five thousand more. ¹⁷The servant who had two thousand coins did the same with his money and earned two thousand more. ¹⁸But the servant with one thousand coins dug a hole and hid his master's money in the ground.

¹⁹Some time later the master of those servants returned. He called them in and asked what they had done with his money. ²⁰The servant who had been given five thousand coins brought them in with the five thousand that he had earned. He said, "Sir, you gave me five thousand coins, and I have earned five thousand more."

²¹"Wonderful!" his master replied. "You are a good and faithful servant. I left you in charge of only a little, but now I will put you in charge of much more. Come and share in my happiness!"

[22]Next, the servant who had been given two thousand coins came in and said, "Sir, you gave me two thousand coins, and I have earned two thousand more."

[23]"Wonderful!" his master replied. "You are a good and faithful servant. I left you in charge of only a little, but now I will put you in charge of much more. Come and share in my happiness!"

[24]The servant who had been given one thousand coins then came in and said, "Sir, I know that you are hard to get along with. You harvest what you don't plant and gather crops where you haven't scattered seed. [25]I was frightened and went out and hid your money in the ground. Here is every single coin!"

[26]The master of the servant told him, "You are lazy and good-for-nothing! You know that I harvest what I don't plant and gather crops where I haven't scattered seed. [27]You could have at least put my money in the bank, so that I could have earned interest on it."

[28]Then the master said, "Now your money will be taken away and given to the servant with ten thousand coins! [29]Everyone who has something will be given more, and they will have more than enough. But everything will be taken from those who don't have anything. [30]You are a worthless servant, and you will be thrown out into the dark where people will cry and grit their teeth in pain."

## The final judgment

Jesus continued:

³¹When the Son of Man comes in his glory with all his angels, he will sit on his royal throne. ³²The people of all nations will be brought before him, and he will separate them, as shepherds separate their sheep from their goats.

³³He will place the sheep on his right and the goats on his left. ³⁴Then the king will say to those on his right, "My father has blessed you! Come and receive the kingdom that was prepared for you before the world was created. ³⁵When I was hungry, you gave me something to eat, and when I was thirsty, you gave me something to drink. When I was a stranger, you welcomed me, ³⁶and when I was naked, you gave me clothes to wear. When I was sick, you took care of me, and when I was in jail, you visited me."

³⁷Then the ones who pleased the Lord will ask, "When did we give you something to eat or drink? ³⁸When did we welcome you as a stranger or give you clothes to wear ³⁹or visit you while you were sick or in jail?"

⁴⁰The king will answer, "Whenever you did it for any of my people, no matter how unimportant they seemed, you did it for me."

⁴¹Then the king will say to those on his left, "Get away from me! You are under God's curse. Go into the everlasting fire prepared for the devil and his angels! ⁴²I was hungry, but you did not give me anything to eat, and I was thirsty, but you did not give me anything to drink. ⁴³I was a stranger, but you did not

welcome me, and I was naked, but you did not give me any clothes to wear. I was sick and in jail, but you did not take care of me."

⁴⁴Then the people will ask, "Lord, when did we fail to help you when you were hungry or thirsty or a stranger or naked or sick or in jail?"

⁴⁵The king will say to them, "Whenever you failed to help any of my people, no matter how unimportant they seemed, you failed to do it for me."

⁴⁶Then Jesus said, "Those people will be punished for ever. But the ones who pleased God will have eternal life."

## The plot to kill Jesus

**26** When Jesus had finished teaching, he told his disciples, ²"You know that two days from now will be Passover. That is when the Son of Man will be handed over to his enemies and nailed to a cross."

³At that time the chief priests and the nation's leaders were meeting at the home of Caiaphas the high priest. ⁴They secretly planned to have Jesus arrested and put to death. ⁵But they said, "We must not do it during Passover, because the people will riot."

## At Bethany

⁶Jesus was in the town of Bethany, eating at the home of Simon, who had leprosy. ⁷A woman came in with a bottle of expensive perfume and poured it on Jesus' head. ⁸But when his disciples saw this, they became angry and complained, "Why

such a waste? ⁹We could have sold this perfume for a lot of money and given it to the poor."

¹⁰Jesus knew what they were thinking, and he said:

Why are you bothering this woman? She has done a beautiful thing for me. ¹¹You will always have the poor with you, but you won't always have me. ¹²She has poured perfume on my body to prepare it for burial. ¹³You may be sure that wherever the good news is told all over the world, people will remember what she has done. And they will tell others.

## Judas and the chief priests

¹⁴Judas Iscariot was one of the twelve disciples. He went to the chief priests ¹⁵and asked, "How much will you give me if I help you arrest Jesus?" They paid Judas thirty silver coins, ¹⁶and from then on he started looking for a good chance to betray Jesus.

## Jesus eats the Passover meal with his disciples

¹⁷On the first day of the Festival of Thin Bread, Jesus' disciples came to him and asked, "Where do you want us to prepare the Passover meal?"

¹⁸Jesus told them to go to a certain man in the city and tell him, "Our teacher says, 'My time has come! I want to eat the Passover meal with my disciples in your home.'" ¹⁹They did as Jesus told them and prepared the meal.

²⁰⁻²¹When Jesus was eating with his twelve disciples that evening, he said, "One of you will hand me over to my enemies."

²²The disciples were very sad, and each one said to Jesus, "Lord, you can't mean me!"

²³He answered, "One of you men who has eaten with me from this dish will betray me. ²⁴The Son of Man will die, as the Scriptures say. But it's going to be terrible for the one who betrays me! That man would be better off if he had never been born."

²⁵Judas said, "Teacher, surely you don't mean me!"

"That's what you say!" Jesus replied. But later, Judas did betray him.

## The Lord's Supper

²⁶During the meal Jesus took some bread in his hands. He blessed the bread and broke it. Then he gave it to his disciples and said, "Take this and eat it. This is my body."

²⁷Jesus picked up a cup of wine and gave thanks to God. He then gave it to his disciples and said, "Take this and drink it. ²⁸This is my blood, and with it God makes his agreement with you. It will be poured out, so that many people will have their sins forgiven. ²⁹From now on I am not going to drink any wine, until I drink new wine with you in my Father's kingdom." ³⁰Then they sang a hymn and went out to the Mount of Olives.

## Peter's promise

³¹Jesus said to his disciples, "During this very night, all of you will reject me, as the Scriptures say,

'I will strike down
    the shepherd,

and the sheep
will be scattered. '

³²But after I am raised to life, I will go to Galilee ahead of you."

³³Peter spoke up, "Even if all the others reject you, I never will!"

³⁴Jesus replied, "I promise you that before a cock crows tonight, you will say three times that you don't know me." ³⁵But Peter said, "Even if I have to die with you, I will never say I don't know you."

All the others said the same thing.

## Jesus prays

³⁶Jesus went with his disciples to a place called Gethsemane. When they got there, he told them, "Sit here while I go over there and pray."

³⁷Jesus took along Peter and the two brothers, James and John. He was very sad and troubled, ³⁸and he said to them, "I am so sad that I feel as if I am dying. Stay here and keep awake with me."

³⁹Jesus walked on a little way. Then he knelt with his face to the ground and prayed, "My Father, if it is possible, don't make me suffer by making me drink from this cup. But do what you want, and not what I want."

⁴⁰He came back and found his disciples sleeping. So he said to Peter, "Can't any of you stay awake with me for just one hour? ⁴¹Stay awake and pray that you won't be tested. You want to do what is right, but you are weak."

⁴²Again Jesus went to pray and said, "My Father, if there is no other way, and I must suffer, I will still do what you want."

⁴³Jesus came back and found them sleeping again. They simply could not keep their eyes open. ⁴⁴He left them and prayed the same prayer once more.

⁴⁵Finally, Jesus returned to his disciples and said, "Are you still sleeping and resting? The time has come for the Son of Man to be handed over to sinners. ⁴⁶Get up! Let's go. The one who will betray me is already here."

## Jesus is arrested

⁴⁷Jesus was still speaking, when Judas the betrayer came up. He was one of the twelve disciples, and a large mob armed with swords and clubs was with him. They had been sent by the chief priests and the nation's leaders. ⁴⁸Judas had told them beforehand, "Arrest the man I greet with a kiss."

⁴⁹Judas walked right up to Jesus and said, "Hello, teacher." Then Judas kissed him.

⁵⁰Jesus replied, "My friend, why are you here?"

The men grabbed Jesus and arrested him. ⁵¹One of Jesus' followers pulled out a sword. He struck the servant of the high priest and cut off his ear.

⁵²But Jesus told him, "Put your sword away. Anyone who lives by fighting will die by fighting. ⁵³Don't you know that I could ask my Father, and straight away he would send me more than twelve armies of angels? ⁵⁴But then, how could the words of the Scriptures come true, which say that this must happen?"

[55]Jesus said to the mob, "Why do you come with swords and clubs to arrest me like a criminal? Day after day I sat and taught in the temple, and you didn't arrest me. [56]But all this happened, so that what the prophets wrote would come true."

All Jesus' disciples left him and ran away.

## Jesus is questioned by the council

[57]After Jesus had been arrested, he was led off to the house of Caiaphas the high priest. The nation's leaders and the teachers of the Law of Moses were meeting there. [58]But Peter followed along at a distance and came to the courtyard of the high priest's palace. He went in and sat down with the guards to see what was going to happen.

[59]The chief priests and the whole council wanted to put Jesus to death. So they tried to find some people who would tell lies about him in court. [60]But they could not find any, even though many did come and tell lies. At last, two men came forward [61]and said, "This man claimed that he would tear down God's temple and build it again in three days."

[62]The high priest stood up and asked Jesus, "Why don't you say something in your own defence? Don't you hear the charges they are making against you?" [63]But Jesus did not answer. So the high priest said, "With the living God looking on, you must tell the truth. Tell us, are you the Messiah, the Son of God?"

[64]"That is what you say!" Jesus answered. "But I tell all of you,

'Soon you will see
the Son of Man
sitting at the right side

of God All-Powerful
and coming on the clouds
of heaven. "

⁶⁵The high priest then tore his robe and said, "This man claims to be God! We don't need any more witnesses! You have heard what he said. ⁶⁶What do you think?"

They answered, "He is guilty and deserves to die!" ⁶⁷Then they spat in his face and hit him with their fists. Others slapped him ⁶⁸and said, "You think you are the Messiah! So tell us who hit you!"

## Peter says he doesn't know Jesus

⁶⁹While Peter was sitting out in the courtyard, a servant girl came up to him and said, "You were with Jesus from Galilee."

⁷⁰But in front of everyone Peter said, "That isn't so! I don't know what you are talking about!"

⁷¹When Peter had gone out to the gate, another servant girl saw him and said to some people there, "This man was with Jesus from Nazareth."

⁷²Again Peter denied it, and this time he swore, "I don't even know that man!"

⁷³A little while later some people standing there walked over to Peter and said, "We know that you are one of them. We can tell it because you talk like someone from Galilee."

⁷⁴Peter began to curse and swear, "I don't know that man!"

At once a cock crowed, ⁷⁵and Peter remembered that Jesus had said, "Before a cock crows, you will say three times that you don't know me." Then Peter went out and cried hard.

## Jesus is taken to Pilate

**27** Early the next morning all the chief priests and the nation's leaders met and decided that Jesus should be put to death. ²They tied him up and led him away to Pilate the governor.

## The death of Judas

³Judas had betrayed Jesus, but when he learnt that Jesus had been sentenced to death, he was sorry for what he had done. He returned the thirty silver coins to the chief priests and leaders ⁴and said, "I have sinned by betraying a man who has never done anything wrong."

"So what? That's your problem, " they replied. ⁵Judas threw the money into the temple and then went out and hanged himself.

⁶The chief priests picked up the money and said, "This money was paid to have a man killed. We can't put it in the temple treasury." ⁷Then they had a meeting and decided to buy a field that belonged to someone who made clay pots. They wanted to use it as a graveyard for foreigners. ⁸That's why people still call that place "Field of Blood".

⁹ So the words of the prophet Jeremiah came true,

"They took
the thirty silver coins,
the price of a person
among the people of Israel.
¹⁰ They paid it

for a potter's field,
as the Lord
had commanded me."

## Pilate questions Jesus

[11]Jesus was brought before Pilate the governor, who asked him, "Are you the king of the Jews?"

"Those are your words!" Jesus answered. [12]And when the chief priests and leaders brought their charges against him, he did not say a thing.

[13]Pilate asked him, "Don't you hear what crimes they say you have done?" [14]But Jesus did not say anything, and the governor was greatly amazed.

## The death sentence

[15]During Passover the governor always freed a prisoner chosen by the people. [16]At that time a well-known terrorist named Jesus Barabbas was in jail. [17]So when the crowd came together, Pilate asked them, "Which prisoner do you want me to set free? Do you want Jesus Barabbas or Jesus who is called the Messiah?" [18]Pilate knew that the leaders had brought Jesus to him because they were jealous.

[19]While Pilate was judging the case, his wife sent him a message. It said, "Don't have anything to do with that innocent man. I have had nightmares because of him."

[20]But the chief priests and the leaders convinced the crowds to ask for Barabbas to be set free and for Jesus to be

killed. [21]Pilate asked the crowd again, "Which of these two men do you want me to set free?"

"Barabbas!" they replied.

[22]Pilate asked them, "What am I to do with Jesus, who is called the Messiah?"

They all yelled, "Nail him to a cross!"

[23]Pilate answered, "But what crime has he done?"

"Nail him to a cross!" they yelled even louder.

[24]Pilate saw that there was nothing he could do and that the people were starting to riot. So he took some water and washed his hands in front of them and said, "I won't have anything to do with killing this man. You are the ones doing it!"

[25]Everyone answered, "We and our own families will take the blame for his death!"

[26]Pilate set Barabbas free. Then he ordered his soldiers to beat Jesus with a whip and nail him to a cross.

## Soldiers make fun of Jesus

[27]The governor's soldiers led Jesus into the fortress and brought together the rest of the troops. [28]They stripped off Jesus' clothes and put a scarlet robe on him. [29]They made a crown out of thorn branches and placed it on his head, and they put a stick in his right hand. The soldiers knelt down and pretended to worship him. They made fun of him and shouted, "Hey, you king of the Jews!" [30]Then they spat on him. They took the stick from him and beat him on the head with it.

## Jesus is nailed to a cross

³¹When the soldiers had finished making fun of Jesus, they took off the robe. They put his own clothes back on him and led him off to be nailed to a cross. ³²On the way they met a man from Cyrene named Simon, and they forced him to carry Jesus' cross.

³³They came to a place named Golgotha, which means "Place of a Skull". ³⁴There they gave Jesus some wine mixed with a drug to ease the pain. But when Jesus tasted what it was, he refused to drink it.

³⁵The soldiers nailed Jesus to a cross and gambled to see who would get his clothes. ³⁶Then they sat down to guard him. ³⁷Above his head they put a sign that told why he was nailed there. It read, "This is Jesus, the King of the Jews." ³⁸The soldiers also nailed two criminals on crosses, one to the right of Jesus and the other to his left.

³⁹People who passed by said terrible things about Jesus. They shook their heads and ⁴⁰shouted, "So you're the one who claimed you could tear down the temple and build it again in three days! If you are God's Son, save yourself and come down from the cross!"

⁴¹The chief priests, the leaders, and the teachers of the Law of Moses also made fun of Jesus. They said, ⁴²"He saved others, but he can't save himself. If he is the king of Israel, he should come down from the cross! Then we will believe him. ⁴³He trusted God, so let God save him, if he wants to. He even said

he was God's Son." ⁴⁴The two criminals also said cruel things to Jesus.

## The death of Jesus

⁴⁵At midday the sky turned dark and stayed that way until three o'clock. ⁴⁶Then about that time Jesus shouted, "Eli, Eli, lema sabachthani?" which means, "My God, my God, why have you deserted me?"

⁴⁷Some of the people standing there heard Jesus and said, "He's calling for Elijah." ⁴⁸One of them at once ran and grabbed a sponge. He soaked it in wine, then put it on a stick and held it up to Jesus.

⁴⁹Others said, "Wait! Let's see if Elijah will come and save him." ⁵⁰Once again Jesus shouted, and then he died.

⁵¹At once the curtain in the temple was torn in two from top to bottom. The earth shook, and rocks split apart. ⁵²Graves opened, and many of God's people were raised to life. ⁵³Then after Jesus had risen to life, they came out of their graves and went into the holy city, where they were seen by many people.

⁵⁴The officer and the soldiers guarding Jesus felt the earthquake and saw everything else that happened. They were frightened and said, "This man really was God's Son!"

⁵⁵Many women had come with Jesus from Galilee to be of help to him, and they were there, looking on at a distance. ⁵⁶Mary Magdalene, Mary the mother of James and Joseph, and the mother of James and John were some of these women.

### Jesus is buried

⁵⁷That evening a rich disciple named Joseph from the town of Arimathea ⁵⁸went and asked for Jesus' body. Pilate gave orders for it to be given to Joseph, ⁵⁹who took the body and wrapped it in a clean linen cloth. ⁶⁰Then Joseph put the body in his own tomb that had been cut into solid rock and had never been used. He rolled a big stone against the entrance to the tomb and went away.

⁶¹All this time Mary Magdalene and the other Mary were sitting across from the tomb.

⁶²On the next day, which was a Sabbath, the chief priests and the Pharisees went together to Pilate. ⁶³They said, "Sir, we remember what that liar said while he was still alive. He claimed that in three days he would come back from death. ⁶⁴So please order the tomb to be carefully guarded for three days. If you don't, his disciples may come and steal his body. They will tell the people that he has been raised to life, and this last lie will be worse than the first one."

⁶⁵Pilate said to them, "All right, take some of your soldiers and guard the tomb as well as you know how." ⁶⁶So they sealed it tight and placed soldiers there to guard it.

### Jesus is alive

**28** The Sabbath was over, and it was almost daybreak on Sunday when Mary Magdalene and the other Mary went to see the tomb. ²Suddenly a strong earthquake struck, and the Lord's angel came down from heaven. He rolled away the stone and sat on it. [3]The angel looked as bright as lightning, and his clothes were white as snow. [4]The guards shook from fear and fell down, as though they were dead.

[5]The angel said to the women, "Don't be afraid! I know you are looking for Jesus, who was nailed to a cross. [6]He isn't here! God has raised him to life, just as Jesus said he would. Come, see the place where his body was lying. [7]Now hurry! Tell his disciples that he has been raised to life and is on his way to Galilee. Go there, and you will see him. That is what I came to tell you."

[8]The women were frightened and yet very happy, as they hurried from the tomb and ran to tell his disciples. [9]Suddenly Jesus met them and greeted them. They went near him, held on to his feet, and worshipped him. [10]Then Jesus said, "Don't be afraid! Tell my followers to go to Galilee. They will see me there."

## Report of the guard

[11]While the women were on their way, some soldiers who had been guarding the tomb went into the city. They told the chief priests everything that had happened. [12]So the chief priests met with the leaders and decided to bribe the soldiers with a lot of money. [13]They said to the soldiers, "Tell everyone that Jesus' disciples came during the night and stole his body while you were asleep. [14]If the governor hears about this, we will talk to him. You won't have anything to worry about." [15]The soldiers took the money and did what they were told. Some of the Jewish people still tell each other this story.

### What Jesus' followers must do

[16]Jesus' eleven disciples went to a mountain in Galilee, where Jesus had told them to meet him. [17]They saw him and worshipped him, but some of them doubted.

[18]Jesus came to them and said:

I have been given all authority in heaven and on earth! [19]Go to the people of all nations and make them my disciples. Baptize them in the name of the Father, the Son, and the Holy Spirit, [20]and teach them to do everything I have told you. I will be with you always, even until the end of the world.

# Xpedition Force memory verses

Work out these verses and where to find them in Xpedition Force Matthew's Story

## Memory verse 1

Solve this code to find the memory verse from Day 1!

[coded symbols line 1]

[coded symbols line 2]

[coded symbols line 3]

Matthew 21:5

_ _ _ _   _ _ _ _   _ _   _ _ _ _ _ _   _ _   _ _ _.   _ _   _ _

_ _ _ _ _ _   _ _ _   _ _ _ _ _   _ _   _   _ _ _ _ _ _.

Matthew 21:5

✔ O   ⁘ R   ✡ K   ↝ Y   ⊙ N   ✏ G   ✻ U   ☀ S   ☼ I
◆ C   ✱ T   ✄ H   ⍝ B   ▭ M   ✗ L   ♣ A   ⊷ D   ✎ E

Which page is it on in Xpedition Force Matthew's Story?

111

## Memory verse 2

Can you complete the verse?

J_s_s s__d, 'I d_dn't c_m_ t_ _nv_t_ g__d p__pl_ t_ b_ my f_ll_w_rs. _ c_m_ t_ _nv_t_ s_nn_rs.'

Matthew 9:13 (page 35)

O_ I△ E△ A⊞ U⊙

## Memory verse 3

Cross out every fourth letter.

JESXUSTXOOKXSOMXEBRXEADXINHXISHXANDXSHEXSAIXD-TAXKETXHISXANDXEATXITTXHISXISMXYBOXDY

_ _ _ _ _  _ _ _ _  _ _ _ _  _ _ _ _  _ _  _ _ _

_ _ _ _ _.  _ _  _ _ _ _,  '_ _ _ _  _ _ _ _  _ _ _  _ _ _

_ _.  _ _ _ _  _ _  _ _  _ _ _ _.'

Matthew 26:26 (page 98)

112

## Memory verse 4

Fill in the missing words.

The _ _ _ of _ _ _ did not come to be a _ _ _ _ _ master, but

a _ _ _ _ _ who will give his _ _ _ _ to rescue many

_ _ _ _ _ _.

Matthew 20:28 (page 75)

## Memory verse 5

Can you work out the code? See the bottom of the page if you need any help!

IDRTR HRM'S GDQD! FNC GZR QZHRDC GHL
SN KHED, ITRS ZR IDRTR RZHC GD VNTKC.

_ _ _ _ _ _ _ _'_ _ _ _ _! _ _ _ _ _ _ _ _ _ _ _ _ _ _ _

_ _ _ _ _ _, _ _ _ _ _ _ _ _ _ _ _ _ _ _ _ _ _ _ _ _.

Matthew 28:6 (page 109)

Each letter in the code stands for the letter after it in the alphabet!

113

# Best-known bits in Matthew

**Visit of the wisemen**  Matthew 2:1–14 (page 12)

**The Sermon on the Mount**  Matthew 5–7 (pages 19–31)
*For example: God blesses those people who depend only on him. They belong to the kingdom of heaven.*

**The Lord's prayer**  Matthew 6:9–13 (page 26)
*Our Father in heaven, help us to honour your name.*

**Jesus said they were not to worry**  Matthew 6:34 (page 28)
*Don't worry about tomorrow. It will take care of itself. You have enough to worry about today.*

**Jesus feeds over 5,000 people**  Matthew 14:13–21 (page 55)

**Jesus walks on water**  Matthew 14:22–32 (page 56)

**Jesus is nailed to a cross**  Matthew 27:31–44 (page 106)

**Jesus comes alive again**  Matthew 28:1–15 (page 108)

# Matthew is for you!!

**When you are being bullied**
Read Matthew 5:11,12 (page 21)

**When you are worried and upset**
Read Matthew 6:34 (page 28)

**When you want to talk with God**
Read Matthew 6:5–15 (page 25)

**When you are afraid**
Read Matthew 10:29–31 (page 40)

**When you are tired**
Read Matthew 11:28–30 (page 44)

**When it feels like children don't matter**
Read Matthew 19:13–15 (page 71)

**When you wonder what's important in life**
Read Matthew 22:37–39 (page 84)

# The best things about Xpedition Force

The funniest thing: _____

The loudest thing: _____

The saddest thing: _____

The bit of the Bible story I most enjoyed: _____

_____

The person in the drama I liked best: _____

Two things I have discovered about Jesus:

1 _____

2 _____


Two things I will remember from Xpedition Force:

1 _____

2 _____